bon appétit

BEST
RECIPES
2015

Edited by Adam Rapoport

Condé Nast
One World Trade Center
New York, New York 10007

www.bonappetit.com

9 8 7 6 5 4 3 2 1

ISBN: 978-0-692-34981-6

Design: Jody Churchfield
Illustrations: Tuan Nini

Front Cover: The New Caprese, p. 46
Back Cover: Barley, Fennel, and Beet Salad;
Bean Salad with Lemon and Herbs, p. 59
Photographer: Christopher Testani
Food Stylist: Rebecca Jurkevich
Prop Stylist: Kaitlyn Du Ross

SOUR
CHERRY PIE
P. 217

contents

introduction

Walk into the *Bon Appétit* Test Kitchen on any given day, and here's what you might see: digital food editor Dawn Perry standing over a pot of onions, trying to extract just the right amount of caramelized goodness from them. A few feet away, senior food editor Alison Roman might be rolling out a pie crust to make the most of summer's bounty of cherries. Meanwhile, food director Carla Lalli Music might be sampling a *labneh* dip that editor Claire Saffitz is refining, positing whether it needs a pinch more Aleppo pepper or just a shot of lemon zest.

Every day, every week, all year long, the cooking and tasting continue. Which is how we manage to develop and test (and re-test) some 40 recipes an issue—about 500 a year.

Some we create on our own, some we harvest from the industry's most accomplished chefs, like London's Yotam Ottolenghi or Jody Williams, who has bustling restaurants in both New York and Paris.

But no matter where the recipes originate, they're all rigorously tested and tasted by a team of editors with equal amounts enthusiasm and heated discussion. Nothing receives the green light till it meets our standards—dishes that we ourselves would be thrilled to cook at home, and that we know will work perfectly every time.

And while all of the recipes measure up, we'll be honest: There are some we love just a bit more than others. Like that batch of golden-brown, batter-dipped fish tacos topped with slaw and brightened with fresh lime juice on page 142. Or the salted-butter apple galette with maple whipped cream on page 229 (good lord!). And don't even get us started on our herbed "faux-tisserie" chicken with potatoes (page 119), a radically simple low-and-slow technique that nets you the moistest, most flavorful chicken you've ever had—restaurants included.

We're talking the best of the best, which is what this book is all about. Some of the recipes are simple and some are ambitious; some are homey and some refined; and some are healthy...while more than a few are indulgent. Along the way, we include tips, techniques, and information on our test kitchen's favorite tools and ingredient discoveries from the past year to help you become an even better, more up-to-date cook. In other words, there is something here for every level and every occasion. We just hope you have as much fun making these recipes as we did testing them.

Adam Rapoport
EDITOR IN CHIEF

1

soups &
salads

_____

SPICY PORK and MUSTARD GREEN SOUP

4 SERVINGS

½ lb. ground pork

2 garlic cloves, finely chopped

2 tsp. finely grated peeled ginger

1 tsp. Sichuan peppercorns, crushed

¾ tsp. crushed red pepper flakes

½ tsp. cumin seeds, coarsely chopped

1 Tbsp. vegetable oil

Kosher salt, freshly ground black pepper

4 cups low-sodium chicken broth

1 bunch mustard greens, torn (about 4 cups)

4 scallions, thinly sliced

2 Tbsp. reduced-sodium soy sauce

1 tsp. fish sauce (such as nam pla or nuoc nam)

8 oz. wide rice noodles

* **ALSO TRY IT WITH:** Beet greens, kale, or turnip greens

It might look like way too much when the mustard greens are raw, but add them all to this hearty, spice-forward soup anyway. As you stir them in, the peppery leaves will quickly wilt down to a silky texture.

Mix pork, garlic, ginger, Sichuan peppercorns, red pepper flakes, and cumin in a medium bowl. Heat oil in a large pot over medium heat. Add pork mixture; season with salt and pepper and cook, stirring and breaking up with a spoon, until browned and cooked through, 8–10 minutes.

Add broth and bring to a boil; reduce heat and simmer until flavors meld, 8–10 minutes. Add mustard greens, scallions, soy sauce, and fish sauce and cook, stirring occasionally, until greens are tender, 5–8 minutes; season with salt and black pepper.

Meanwhile, cook noodles according to package directions; drain.

Divide noodles among bowls and ladle soup over.

You're much more likely to cook your greens if the prep work is already done. So when you bring them home from the market, immediately strip the leaves off the stems, wash and thoroughly dry them, and refrigerate in a plastic bag with a sheet of dry paper towel inside. They'll keep for several days this way.

GREEN GARLIC and PEA SOUP with WHIPPED CREAM

4 SERVINGS

2 bunches green garlic (about 1 lb.)

4 Tbsp. olive oil, divided

Kosher salt, freshly ground black pepper

2 cups shelled fresh peas (from about 2 lb. pods) or frozen peas, thawed

⅓ cup heavy cream

The key to a vibrant green (not khaki) soup: Bring the water up to a boil quickly over high heat, and err on undercooking the peas to preserve their color.

Cut dark-green tops from green garlic and slice crosswise ½" thick; slice bulbs and pale-green stalks crosswise ¼" thick.

Heat 2 Tbsp. oil in a large saucepan over medium heat. Add bulbs and stalks, season with salt and pepper, and cook, stirring often, until beginning to soften, 8–10 minutes. Add tops and cook, stirring often, until soft, about 3 minutes.

Add 4 cups water to saucepan and bring to a boil. Add peas, reduce heat, and simmer gently until peas are bright green and tender, about 5 minutes.

Let cool slightly, then purée soup in a blender with remaining 2 Tbsp. oil, adding water to thin if needed, until smooth. Strain soup through a fine-mesh sieve into a clean saucepan, pressing on solids; season with salt and pepper. Reheat briefly (to preserve color) before serving.

Beat cream with a whisk in a medium bowl to soft peaks; season with salt and pepper. Serve soup with a swirl of whipped cream.

DO AHEAD: Soup can be made 1 day ahead. Cover and chill.

Substitute green garlic (also called spring garlic) in recipes for onions, scallions, or leeks. The tender cloves don't need to be peeled before chopping.

QUICK and EASY PORK PHO

8 SERVINGS

1 medium onion, peeled,
   halved through root end

2 chiles de árbol or ½ tsp.
   crushed red pepper flakes

2 garlic cloves, crushed

1 cinnamon stick

2 star anise pods

1 tsp. fennel seeds

1 1" piece ginger, peeled, crushed

8 cups low-sodium chicken broth

2 Tbsp. vegetable oil

2 bone-in pork shoulder steaks
   (about 12 oz. each)

   Kosher salt, freshly
   ground black pepper

8 oz. thin rice stick noodles

   Mung bean sprouts, fresh
   cilantro leaves with
   tender stems, thinly sliced
   scallions, chopped
   unsalted, roasted peanuts,
   and lime wedges
   (for serving)

You don't have to simmer all day to get the warm, rich flavor of this classic, brothy Vietnamese pork soup. Charring an onion in a dry skillet and adding a few spices transforms store-bought broth into something deeply satisfying. Put out all the toppings to let everyone customize his or her bowl.

Heat a dry large cast-iron skillet over medium-high. Cook onion, cut side down, until lightly charred, about 5 minutes; transfer to a plate.

Add chiles (if using crushed red pepper flakes, add with fennel seeds), garlic, cinnamon stick, and star anise to skillet and cook, stirring, until fragrant, about 1 minute. Add fennel seeds and cook, stirring, until fragrant, about 20 seconds (do not burn). Quickly transfer to a large saucepan (reserve skillet) and add onion, ginger, and broth; bring to a boil. Reduce heat and simmer until broth is flavorful.

Meanwhile, heat oil in reserved skillet over medium-high heat. Season pork with salt and pepper and cook until browned and cooked through, about 4 minutes per side. Transfer to a cutting board and let rest 5 minutes before thinly slicing.

Cook noodles according to package directions. Divide among bowls; add pork. Strain broth and ladle into bowls. Top pho with bean sprouts, cilantro, scallions, and peanuts and serve with lime wedges.

LEEK SOUP with SHOESTRING POTATOES and FRIED HERBS

8 SERVINGS

SOUP

½ cup (1 stick) unsalted butter

6 large leeks, white and pale-green parts only, halved lengthwise, thinly sliced crosswise

1 small onion, thinly sliced

5 garlic cloves, thinly sliced

Kosher salt

2 cups whole milk, divided

1 cup heavy cream, divided

1 cup plain whole-milk yogurt, divided

Freshly ground black pepper

POTATOES AND ASSEMBLY

1 russet potato, peeled, cut into thin matchsticks

Vegetable oil (for frying; about 4 cups)

¼ cup fresh flat-leaf parsley leaves

1 sprig rosemary

Kosher salt

Flaky sea salt (such as Maldon)

SPECIAL EQUIPMENT: A deep-fry thermometer

For Portland, Oregon, chef Naomi Pomeroy's beautiful, almost bone-white soup, don't let the leeks and onion take on any color as they soften. If you want an extra-refined texture, strain the soup through a fine-mesh sieve.

SOUP

Melt butter in a large heavy pot over medium heat. Add leeks, onion, and garlic and season with salt. Cook, stirring often, until vegetables begin to soften, 5–7 minutes. Add 1 cup water and cook, stirring occasionally, until vegetables are very soft, 25–30 minutes. Let cool slightly, then transfer half of leek mixture to a blender and add half of milk, cream, and yogurt. Purée until very smooth; pour into a large bowl. Repeat with remaining leek mixture, milk, cream, and yogurt.

Return soup to pot and heat over medium, adding water by ¼-cupfuls, until soup is thick enough to hold potatoes without sinking but thin enough that a spoon dragged across the top doesn't leave a trail. Season with salt and pepper.

DO AHEAD: Soup can be made 2 days ahead. Cover and chill.

POTATOES AND ASSEMBLY

Rinse potato matchsticks in a colander under cold water until water runs clear; pat completely dry.

Fit a medium saucepan with thermometer; pour in oil to measure 2". Heat over medium-high until thermometer registers 350°. Working in batches and returning oil to 350° between batches, add potato by the handful and fry, turning occasionally, until golden and crisp, about 2 minutes. Using a spider or slotted spoon, transfer potato to paper towels to drain. Fry parsley and rosemary until parsley is translucent, about 15 seconds. Add to potato and let cool; season with kosher salt. Serve soup topped with a nest of potatoes and herbs and seasoned with sea salt.

DO AHEAD: Potatoes and herbs can be fried 2 hours ahead. Store uncovered at room temperature.

COLLARD GREEN
SALAD with CASHEWS
and LIME

4 SERVINGS

1 cup unsalted, roasted
  cashews, divided

4 Tbsp. finely grated Pecorino,
  divided, plus shaved for
  serving

  Kosher salt, freshly ground
  black pepper

1 anchovy fillet packed in oil,
  drained, finely chopped

¼ cup olive oil

2 Tbsp. fresh lime juice

1 tsp. pink peppercorns, crushed,
  plus more for serving

½ bunch collard greens, ribs
  and stems removed, leaves
  coarsely torn

* **ALSO TRY IT WITH:** Tuscan kale

Sturdy greens demand big flavors, like the cheese, rich nuts, and anchovies in this healthy-yet-decadent salad. Raw collards have some chew to them, so use your hands to work the dressing into the leaves until they soften and start to wilt. This is also a great technique to try on kale.

Process ½ cup cashews, 2 Tbsp. grated Pecorino, and 3 Tbsp. water in a food processor, thinning with more water as needed, until a smooth, creamy paste forms; season with salt and black pepper. Set cashew paste aside.

Whisk anchovy, oil, lime juice, 1 tsp. pink peppercorns, and 2 Tbsp. grated Pecorino in a large bowl; season with salt and black pepper. Coarsely chop remaining ½ cup cashews. Add nuts and collard greens to large bowl and toss to coat, gently massaging dressing into leaves with your fingers to bruise and slightly wilt.

Spread some reserved cashew paste onto each plate and top with salad and shaved Pecorino; sprinkle with more crushed pink peppercorns.

ARUGULA, APPLE, and PARSNIP with BUTTERMILK DRESSING

8 SERVINGS

¼ cup buttermilk

4 Tbsp. olive oil, divided

Kosher salt, freshly ground black pepper

1 large Pink Lady apple, cored, thinly sliced

1 small parsnip, peeled, thinly sliced lengthwise on a mandoline

1 bunch arugula, tough stems trimmed

¼ cup fresh dill with tender stems

2 Tbsp. apple cider vinegar

Flaky sea salt (such as Maldon)

Parsnip, a vegetable that's best known roasted or puréed, is crunchy, sweet, and delicious when served raw and thinly sliced. We love the way it complements the shaved apple in this fall-friendly salad.

Whisk buttermilk and 2 Tbsp. oil in a small bowl; season dressing with kosher salt and pepper.

Toss apple, parsnip, arugula, and dill in a large bowl. Drizzle salad with vinegar and toss to coat; season with kosher salt, pepper, and more vinegar, if desired.

Spoon half of dressing onto serving plates or a large platter. Add remaining 2 Tbsp. oil to salad and toss to coat. Mound salad on top of dressing. Spoon remaining dressing over and season with sea salt.

DO AHEAD: Dressing can be made 2 days ahead. Cover and chill.

GRILLED LETTUCES
with CRÈME FRAÎCHE
and AVOCADO

4 SERVINGS

2 romaine lettuce hearts and/or
   large heads of Treviso
   radicchio, halved lengthwise

3 Tbsp. olive oil, divided,
   plus more

   Kosher salt, freshly
   ground black pepper

1 cup mizuna or baby
   mustard greens

½ cup crème fraîche

1 avocado, cut into quarters

2 Tbsp. fresh lemon juice

   Flaky sea salt (such as Maldon)

Yes, you can grill lettuce. "But don't try this with iceberg," advises Carlo Mirarchi, chef of Roberta's in Bushwick, Brooklyn. Flavorful, robust lettuces work best in this recipe, allowing you to get grill marks on one side while the rest wilts for a surprising new texture combination.

Prepare grill for medium-high heat. Brush cut sides of lettuce with a total of 2 Tbsp. oil; season with kosher salt and pepper. Grill lettuce, cut side down, until lightly charred, about 2 minutes.

Toss mizuna with 1 Tbsp. oil in a medium bowl; season with kosher salt.

Dollop crème fraîche on a platter and top with grilled lettuce and avocado; scatter mizuna over. Drizzle with lemon juice and more oil; season with sea salt and pepper.

THE RESTAURANT BEHIND THE RECIPE
Roberta's

If there's one restaurant that everyone at *Bon Appétit* can agree on, it's Roberta's. When we relaunched the magazine in 2011, we held our first dinner for the new staff there. And it just keeps getting better. The truly D.I.Y. Brooklyn compound started as a pizzeria in a garage in a then-iffy neighborhood. Once the gas got turned on, self-taught chef Carlo Mirarchi started serving food that had chefs like Eric Ripert parking at the picnic tables for produce-driven dishes that were rebellious in their restraint. Whatever Mirarchi and his partners Brandon Hoy and Chris Parachini dreamed up, they made happen, Peter Pan–style: Put an all-food radio station in a shipping container and plant veggies on top? Turn a vacant lot into a motocross track? Set up a tiki bar, then open Blanca, a 12-stool fine-dining restaurant? They make it look fun. And it is. What we really love is the food: brave new meats (braised lamb breast, 21-day dry-aged duck, Wagyu flank steak), heartbreakingly delicate pastas, out-there-yet-hyper-local vegetables (coffee-roasted beets with sunchoke), and *crudo* of Japanese purity. And, yes, we also love the pizzas (and their names). Where else could you order a Tonya Charding pie, some house-made charcuterie, a few Michelin-worthy dishes, and a Rye & Goslings cocktail? We can't wait to go back.

RADICCHIO SALAD with SOURDOUGH DRESSING

4 SERVINGS

3 oz. sourdough bread, crust removed, torn into small pieces (about 1 cup), divided

1 Tbsp. plus ⅓ cup olive oil

Kosher salt, freshly ground black pepper

1 small garlic clove

2 Tbsp. red wine vinegar

1 tsp. Dijon mustard

1 tsp. sugar

1 head radicchio, leaves separated, torn if large

2 scallions, thinly sliced

Here's a new idea for leftover sourdough: Use that bread to enrich your salad dressing. The result is surprisingly creamy and tangy—with the kind of body that makes you think you'd added an egg yolk.

Preheat oven to 425°. Toss half of bread with 1 Tbsp. oil on a rimmed baking sheet; season with salt and pepper. Bake, tossing once, until golden brown, 8–10 minutes.

Pulse garlic, vinegar, mustard, sugar, remaining bread, and 2 Tbsp. water in a blender to combine; let sit 5 minutes to soften bread. With motor running, gradually add remaining ⅓ cup oil; blend until smooth (bread will blend into dressing, thickening and flavoring it, while retaining some texture), about 2 minutes; season with salt and pepper.

Toss radicchio, scallions, croutons, and dressing in a large bowl; season with salt and pepper.

Using a blender rather than a food processor yields a smooth dressing and whips in air for a light texture.

FRIED EGGPLANT,
TOMATO, AND
CUCUMBER SALAD
P. 30

FRIED EGGPLANT, TOMATO, and CUCUMBER SALAD

6 SERVINGS

½ cup fresh cilantro leaves with tender stems

½ cup fresh flat-leaf parsley leaves with tender stems

1 garlic clove, chopped

2 small green chiles, such as Thai, seeds removed, chopped, divided

½ cup olive oil, divided

¾ tsp. kosher salt, plus more

¾ cup plain whole-milk Greek yogurt

1 Tbsp. fresh lemon juice

2 medium eggplants (about 1½ lb.), cut into 1½" pieces

Vegetable oil (for frying; about 2 cups)

1 lb. small tomatoes (about 8), cut into wedges

½ lb. Persian cucumbers (about 3), sliced

SPECIAL EQUIPMENT: A deep-fry thermometer

Eggplant is like a sponge. Salting it draws out moisture and firms up the flesh, and deep-frying ensures it cooks evenly until creamy throughout. Yotam Ottolenghi's version is worth your time.

Purée cilantro, parsley, garlic, half of chiles, and ¼ cup olive oil in a blender or food processor until very smooth; season herb oil with salt and set aside.

Whisk yogurt, lemon juice, and remaining ¼ cup olive oil in a small bowl; season with salt and set yogurt sauce aside.

Place eggplants in a colander set in the sink; season with ¾ tsp. salt. Let sit 30 minutes to drain, then pat dry.

Fit a medium pot with thermometer; pour in vegetable oil to measure 2". Heat over medium-high heat until thermometer registers 375°.

Working in batches and returning oil to 375° between batches, fry eggplants, turning often, until golden brown and tender, about 5 minutes. Using a slotted spoon, transfer eggplants to paper towels to drain; season with salt. Let cool.

Combine eggplants in a large bowl with tomatoes, cucumbers, and remaining chiles; drizzle with some reserved herb oil and toss to combine. Season salad with salt.

Spoon reserved yogurt sauce onto a platter, top with salad, and drizzle with more herb oil.

DO AHEAD: Herb oil and yogurt sauce can be made 1 day ahead. Cover and chill separately.

The Ottolenghi Bibliography

London chef Yotam Ottolenghi has been changing the way we cook, one book at a time, with his vibrant, modern, Middle Eastern-inspired food.

PLENTY:
Vibrant Vegetable Recipes from London's Ottolenghi (2011)

The book that launched the cult. The recipes not only made vegetarian food sexy (note: Ottolenghi wants you to know he loves meat), they also made Western cooks crave Eastern Mediterranean flavors.

OUR FAVORITE RECIPES:
Caramelized Garlic Tart, Shakshuka, Green Pancakes with Lime Butter

JERUSALEM:
A Cookbook (2012)

Both Ottolenghi and his Palestinian executive chef, Sami Tamimi, were born there, albeit on different sides. In this book, they explore the cuisine and cultures of their homeland, adding their own spin.

OUR FAVORITE RECIPES:
Musabaha and Toasted Pita, Jerusalem Mixed Grill, Na'ama's Fattoush

OTTOLENGHI:
The Cookbook (2013)

The Ottolenghi-Tamimi emphasis on freshness and herbs, plus layered textures and flavors, is all here, with a tiny bit of meat—not to mention fantastic desserts.

OUR FAVORITE RECIPES:
Beef and Lamb Meatballs Baked in Tahini, Pistachio and Rose Water Meringues

PLENTY MORE:
Vibrant Vegetable Cooking from London's Ottolenghi (2014)

We're in love with all the fresh combinations— and, of course, ideas for eggplant in his most recent bestseller.

OUR FAVORITE RECIPES:
Haricots Verts and Freekeh with Minty Tahini Dressing; Tomato, Onion, and Roasted Lemon Salad; Halvah Ice Cream with Chocolate Sauce and Roasted Peanuts

SUMMER SQUASH SLAW
with FETA and
TOASTED BUCKWHEAT

4 SERVINGS

¼ cup buckwheat groats

1½ lb. yellow summer squash, julienned on a mandoline or with a knife

2 scallions, thinly sliced

¼ cup coarsely chopped fresh mint

1 tsp. coarsely chopped fresh marjoram or oregano

3 Tbsp. olive oil

1 Tbsp. fresh lemon juice

Kosher salt, freshly ground black pepper

4 oz. feta, thinly sliced

Cooked summer squash can be mushy. Solution: Eat it raw. If you can't find buckwheat groats, use chopped toasted almonds instead.

Toast buckwheat in a dry large skillet over medium-high heat, tossing often, until fragrant, about 4 minutes. Transfer to a plate; let cool.

Toss squash, scallions, mint, marjoram, oil, and lemon juice in a large bowl; season with salt, pepper, and more lemon juice, if desired. Add feta and toasted buckwheat and toss gently to combine.

DO AHEAD: Buckwheat can be toasted 2 days ahead. Store airtight at room temperature.

Toasted whole grains and seeds are a delicious way to add texture, flavor, and nutrition to a dish. Try sprinkling them on soups, salads, even pasta.

CITRUS SALAD with FENNEL VINAIGRETTE

8 SERVINGS

This juicy and bracing salad, from chef Dan Kluger in New York City, gets its crunch from granola-ish sesame clusters. Think of them as seedy croutons. We also love to sprinkle them on grain bowls.

SESAME CLUSTERS

- 1 large egg white
- 3 Tbsp. sugar
- ½ tsp. kosher salt
- ¼ tsp. ground cinnamon
- ¼ tsp. ground cloves
- ¼ tsp. ground nutmeg
- 1 cup sesame seeds

DRESSING AND SALAD

- ⅓ cup olive oil
- ¼ small fennel bulb, finely chopped, plus ½ cup chopped fronds
- 1 small shallot, finely chopped
- 2 Tbsp. finely chopped peeled ginger
- 1 tsp. fennel seeds, crushed
- ¼ cup white wine vinegar
- 2 Tbsp. honey
  Kosher salt and freshly ground black pepper
- 4 navel oranges, blood oranges, tangerines, and/or grapefruit
- 10 cups mixed hardy salad greens (such as radicchio, frisée, and/or endive; about 1 lb.)
- 1 cup fresh flat-leaf parsley leaves

SESAME CLUSTERS

Preheat oven to 350°. Whisk egg white in a small bowl until slightly foamy; whisk in sugar, salt, cinnamon, cloves, and nutmeg. Add sesame seeds and toss to coat.

Spoon sesame mixture in clumps on a parchment-lined baking sheet and bake, stirring occasionally, until golden brown, 10–12 minutes. Let cool.

DO AHEAD: Sesame clusters can be made 1 week ahead. Store airtight at room temperature.

DRESSING AND SALAD

Heat oil in a medium skillet over medium heat. Add chopped fennel, shallot, ginger, and fennel seeds and cook, stirring often, until tender (do not let brown), 8–10 minutes. Mix in vinegar and honey. Let cool; season with salt and pepper.

Finely grate 1 tsp. zest from 1 orange; set aside. Using a sharp knife, cut all peel and white pith from all oranges; discard. Cut between membranes to release segments into a medium bowl; discard membranes.

Toss greens, parsley, fennel fronds, oranges, and dressing in a large bowl. Serve topped with sesame clusters and reserved orange zest.

DO AHEAD: Dressing can be made 1 day ahead. Cover and chill.

ENDIVE SALAD with TOASTED WALNUTS and BREADCRUMBS

4 SERVINGS

½ cup raw walnuts

1 cup coarsely torn fresh breadcrumbs

6 Tbsp. olive oil, divided

Kosher salt

4 anchovy fillets packed in oil, drained, finely chopped

1 garlic clove, finely grated

2 Tbsp. red wine vinegar

Freshly ground black pepper

2 oz. Taleggio cheese, cut into ½" pieces (about ¼ cup)

2 oz. Pecorino duro or Parmesan, broken into ½" pieces (about ¼ cup)

4 endives, sliced crosswise 1" thick

1 tsp. finely grated orange zest

2 Tbsp. fresh orange juice

1 Tbsp. white wine vinegar or white balsamic vinegar

Ignacio Mattos, chef of New York City's Estela, says to get both the walnuts and the breadcrumbs very toasty and dark brown; he loves the contrast between the rich, crunchy, almost burned bits and the endive on top, which gets brightened with both orange juice and zest.

Preheat oven to 350°. Toast walnuts on a rimmed baking sheet, tossing occasionally, until fragrant and slightly darker, 8–10 minutes. Let cool.

Toss breadcrumbs with 2 Tbsp. oil on a clean rimmed baking sheet; season with salt. Bake, tossing once, until golden brown and crisp, 12–15 minutes; let cool.

Mix anchovies, garlic, red wine vinegar, and remaining 4 Tbsp. oil in a medium bowl just to combine; season with salt and pepper. Add toasted walnuts, breadcrumbs, Taleggio, and Pecorino and toss to combine.

Toss endive, orange zest, orange juice, and white wine vinegar in another medium bowl; season with salt and pepper.

Divide walnut mixture among plates and top with endive salad.

DO AHEAD: Vinaigrette can be made 1 day ahead; cover and chill. Walnuts and breadcrumbs can be toasted 1 day ahead; store airtight at room temperature.

THAI DUCK and GRAPEFRUIT SALAD

4 SERVINGS

1 12-oz. duck breast

Kosher salt and freshly ground black pepper

1 garlic clove, finely grated

2 Tbsp. olive oil

1 Tbsp. fish sauce

1 Tbsp. fresh lemon juice

2 tsp. grated peeled ginger

½ tsp. sugar

2 scallions, thinly sliced

2 cups cilantro sprigs

1 cup fresh mint leaves

2 red or pink grapefruits, peeled and white pith removed, cut into segments

Salads don't have to be about the lettuce. This vibrant, Thai-accented salad gets its greens from flavorful herbs, while tangy-sweet grapefruit plays off rich seared duck.

Season duck breast with salt and pepper and cook in a skillet to medium-rare (see below); let rest, then thinly slice.

Whisk garlic, oil, fish sauce, lemon juice, ginger, and sugar in a large bowl; add duck, scallions, cilantro sprigs, mint leaves, and grapefruit segments and toss.

Duck Breast Basics

They may not be in your regular dinner rotation, but cooking duck breasts doesn't require a special occasion. Start them skin side down to slowly render the fat and crisp the skin, then finish briefly on the other side.

1

SCORE IT

Score the fat in a crosshatch pattern, which will help it to render. Cut all the way down to the flesh, taking care not to slash into the meat itself.

2

RENDER IT

Place the duck in a preheated pan over medium heat, flesh side up. You may need to drain off the drippings periodically so the breast doesn't start to shallow-fry.

3

FLIP IT

Once the skin side is crisp and dark golden, turn the breast to sear the flesh side, about 15 minutes total for a perfect medium-rare. Let rest at least 10 minutes before slicing.

KALE with POMEGRANATE DRESSING and RICOTTA SALATA

8 SERVINGS

1 small shallot, finely chopped

2 Tbsp. white wine vinegar

2 tsp. pomegranate molasses

Kosher salt, freshly ground black pepper

1 bunch red Russian or purple kale or 2 bunches Tuscan kale, ribs and stems removed, leaves torn into 2" pieces

½ cup pomegranate seeds

2 Tbsp. olive oil

2 oz. ricotta salata (salted dry ricotta)

Yes, the ubiquitous kale salad has gotten even better! If you can't find *ricotta salata,* try shavings of Manchego, Parmesan, or sharp aged cheddar—anything with a nice balance of rich, salty, and tangy.

Combine shallot, vinegar, and pomegranate molasses in a large bowl; season dressing with salt and pepper and let sit 5 minutes.

Add kale to dressing, season with salt and pepper, and massage dressing into leaves. Add pomegranate seeds and oil and toss to combine. Serve topped with ricotta salata.

DO AHEAD: Dressing can be made 4 hours ahead; cover and chill.

GRAPEFRUIT
AND WHITE BEETS
WITH YOGURT
AND TARRAGON
P. 45

opposite:
STEAK SALAD
WITH CARAWAY
VINAIGRETTE AND
RYE CROUTONS
P. 44

STEAK SALAD with CARAWAY VINAIGRETTE and RYE CROUTONS

4 SERVINGS

- 2 slices seeded rye bread, torn into ¼" pieces
- 3 Tbsp. plus ¼ cup olive oil, divided
- 1½ lb. hanger steak, center membrane removed, cut into 4 pieces
- Kosher salt, freshly ground black pepper
- 1 tsp. caraway seeds
- 2 Tbsp. Sherry vinegar
- 1 Tbsp. whole grain mustard
- ½ tsp. honey
- 4 small carrots, peeled, shaved lengthwise with a vegetable peeler
- 4 cups mustard greens, ribs removed, leaves torn into bite-size pieces
- 1 cup fresh flat-leaf parsley leaves with tender stems

All the flavors of a steak sandwich on rye, but in salad form.

Preheat oven to 400°. Toss bread with 2 Tbsp. oil on a rimmed baking sheet and toast, tossing halfway through, until golden brown, 8–10 minutes; set aside.

Meanwhile, heat 1 Tbsp. oil in a large skillet over medium-high heat. Season steak with salt and pepper and cook, turning occasionally, 8–10 minutes for medium-rare. Transfer to a cutting board; let rest 5 minutes before slicing.

Toast caraway seeds in a small dry skillet over medium heat, tossing, until fragrant, about 2 minutes. Let cool.

Whisk caraway, vinegar, mustard, honey, and remaining ¼ cup oil in a large bowl; season with salt and pepper. Add carrots, mustard greens, parsley, and steak and toss. Serve salad topped with reserved croutons.

DO AHEAD: Vinaigrette can be made 2 days ahead; cover and chill. Croutons can be made 1 day ahead. Store airtight at room temperature.

GRAPEFRUIT and WHITE BEETS with YOGURT and TARRAGON

4 SERVINGS

3 Tbsp. pine nuts

4 medium white or Chioggia (candy-stripe) beets (about 1 lb.)

1 Tbsp. olive oil

Kosher salt

2 Tbsp. white wine vinegar

2 white grapefruits

¾ cup plain Greek yogurt

¼ cup fresh tarragon leaves

Rather than fussily cutting the grapefruit into neat segments for this elegant winter composition, Ignacio Mattos of Estela in New York City cuts them crosswise into disks; he likes the slightly bitter flavor of the membrane itself.

Preheat oven to 350°. Toast pine nuts on a rimmed baking sheet, tossing occasionally, until golden brown, 6–8 minutes; let cool.

Increase oven heat to 400°. Place beets on a sheet of parchment paper set on top of a sheet of foil; rub beets with oil and season with salt. Close up parchment and foil around beets. Place packet on a baking sheet and roast beets until tender, 40–50 minutes. Unwrap beets and let cool.

Peel beets and thinly slice into rounds. Toss beets and vinegar in a medium bowl; season with salt and let stand 15 minutes.

Meanwhile, finely grate ½ tsp. zest from 1 grapefruit and set aside. Using a sharp, small knife, cut all peel and white pith from both grapefruits; discard. Thinly slice grapefruit into rounds.

Place yogurt in a small bowl; season with salt and mix well. Spoon onto plates. Top yogurt with beets and sliced grapefruit, then tarragon, toasted pine nuts, and reserved grapefruit zest.

DO AHEAD: Beets can be roasted 2 days ahead; let cool. Cover and chill. Pine nuts can be toasted 1 day ahead; store airtight at room temperature.

THE RESTAURANT BEHIND THE RECIPE

Estela

Since its opening in 2013, Estela, a so-dimly-lit-you-can't-Instagram-it spot in New York City's Nolita neighborhood, has become an unofficial canteen for *Bon Appétit*'s editors. There, via a menu that meanders through Spain, Italy, and points beyond, we find inspiration in Ignacio Mattos's unexpected flavors and deceptively simple plating. It's easy to rave about perfectly cooked steak (which he boldly serves with anchovy). But our next-day recaps always come back to the salads: We admire how Mattos unlocks the potential of even the humblest ingredients. Even his winter salads—crisp, often all-white affairs—are smart (and delicious) works of art.

The NEW CAPRESE

Done right, the *caprese* salad's timeless combination of tomatoes, fresh mozzarella, and basil is more than the sum of its parts. That's why every component counts: You must seek out the best ingredients, use your fanciest olive oil, and sprinkle on the Maldon salt and coarsely ground black pepper. Master these essentials and the *caprese* formula can be endlessly (and brilliantly) adapted, as seen here.

1	2	3	4	5
THE ORIGINAL: TOMATO	PEACH	CANTALOUPE	GRILLED EGGPLANT	ROASTED RED PEPPER
+	+	+	+	+
MOZZARELLA	BURRATA	SCAMORZA	RICOTTA SALATA	FETA
+	+	+	+	+
BASIL	TARRAGON	MINT	DILL	CHIVE

The easiest way to slice a tomato or ripe, juicy fruit? Use a basic serrated knife. It does a fine job cutting through the delicate skin and flesh of the tomato without smushing it.

1

2

3

4

5

RADICCHIO and APPLE SALAD with PARMESAN CRISPS

8 SERVINGS

6 oz. Parmesan, finely grated, divided

2 Tbsp. honey

½ small shallot, finely chopped

⅓ cup olive oil

3 Tbsp. white wine vinegar

1 tsp. Dijon mustard

Kosher salt, freshly ground black pepper

2 medium heads of radicchio, leaves separated, torn in half if large

1 medium bunch arugula, tough stems removed

1 large Pink Lady apple, thinly sliced

Flaky sea salt (such as Maldon)

Naomi Pomeroy, the chef and owner of Beast restaurant and Expatriate bar in Portland, Oregon, prefers to serve salad at the end of the meal; with this one, you get a bit of a cheese course at the same time.

Preheat oven to 350°. On a silicone mat–lined baking sheet, divide 4 oz. grated Parmesan into 8 mounds. (Alternatively, line with parchment paper and coat with nonstick spray.) Press with your fingers to flatten. Bake until cheese is golden and melted, 6–8 minutes. Transfer baking sheet to a wire rack and let cool; break crisps into coarse pieces.

Heat honey in a small skillet over medium heat until warmed through. Whisk honey, shallot, oil, vinegar, and mustard in a large bowl; season with kosher salt and pepper.

Add radicchio, arugula, apple, and remaining grated Parmesan to vinaigrette; toss to coat. Season with sea salt and pepper. Serve topped with crisps.

DO AHEAD: Vinaigrette and Parmesan crisps (do not break) can be made 1 day ahead. Cover and chill vinaigrette. Keep crisps airtight at room temperature. Reheat until sizzling, if needed, to recrisp.

TOMATO, PICKLED
MELON, AND
BURRATA SALAD
P. 52

TOMATO, PICKLED MELON, and BURRATA SALAD

4 SERVINGS

2 Tbsp. white wine vinegar

½ tsp. kosher salt

¼ tsp. freshly ground black pepper, plus more

1 lb. Sharlyn or Galia melon, rind removed, unseeded, sliced into thin rounds

1 large heirloom tomato, sliced

12 oz. fresh burrata or mozzarella, torn

Olive oil (for drizzling)

Fresh basil leaves (for serving)

Flaky sea salt (such as Maldon)

The classic *caprese* salad just got even better: Ultra-creamy *burrata* replaces mozzarella, and quick-pickled melon adds a sweet acidic twist. If it seems strange to leave in the melon seeds, keep in mind that the flesh immediately surrounding the seeds is the most succulent part of any melon. For those of you who haven't tried eating the crunchy seeds before, hold on to your hats.

Combine vinegar, kosher salt, ¼ tsp. pepper, and 2 Tbsp. water in a large bowl; add melon and toss to coat. Let stand at room temperature at least 30 minutes.

Remove melon from pickling liquid and arrange on a platter with tomato and burrata. Drizzle with oil and some pickling liquid, top with basil, and season with sea salt and pepper.

DO AHEAD: Melon can be pickled 2 hours ahead. Cover and chill.

A Few More Good Melons

Watermelon, cantaloupe, and honeydew might be the easiest melons to find, but grab one of these lesser-known varieties from the farmers' market and you're in for a sweet surprise.

CASABA
The flavor of this wrinkly, ridged gourd recalls cucumber more than the sweeter muskmelons. With a squeeze of citrus juice, it's nice in gazpacho or a smoothie.

CHRISTMAS/SANTA CLAUS
This dark green, oblong melon is available into December. It's on the milder side: Heavy ones will be sweeter. Serve at room temperature with creamy cheeses and cured meats.

PERSIAN
Don't let the musky scent put you off—this melon's orange flesh is as irresistible as a perfect cantaloupe. Often picked too soon, so choose more perfumed ones with tanner skin.

SPRITE
This petite, smooth-skinned type from North Carolina has notes of honeydew, watermelon, and pear. Its uniquely crisp, apple-like flesh makes it easy to dice into an herby, citrusy melon salsa.

CRENSHAW
This cross between a casaba and a Persian comes in both white and green varieties. It's exceptionally luscious, juicy, and a little peppery at its peak; use interchangeably with cantaloupe.

CANARY
At its best, this bright yellow, football-shaped melon is sugary, a little tangy, somewhat tropical-tasting. Great in cold soups or salads, and with herbs such as basil, mint, and cilantro.

CHARENTAIS
Also known as French cantaloupe; honeyed and tender with green ribbing and slight netting (like a cantaloupe with stripes). Extremely fragrant when fully ripe. Keep it simple: Slice and eat.

GALIA
A cantaloupe-honeydew hybrid with delicious-smelling pale green flesh. Extra delectable served chilled with a sprinkling of sea salt.

SHARLYN
A highly perishable variety with a subtle flavor. It's excellent with tangy ingredients like yogurt and goat cheese, or for balancing chile-spiked dishes.

BLACK and WILD RICE SALAD with ROASTED SQUASH

8 SERVINGS

1½ cups black rice

½ cup wild rice

Kosher salt

½ medium butternut squash, peeled, seeds removed, cut into pieces

½ cup olive oil, divided

Freshly ground black pepper

¼ cup red wine vinegar

2 tsp. honey

2 scallions, thinly sliced

1 cup pomegranate seeds

1 cup microgreens or sprouts

½ cup roasted pistachios, chopped

* **ALSO TRY IT WITH:** Any grain (except amaranth)

Start treating grains as a building block for salads, and weeknight meals become effortless. Simply add raw and/or cooked vegetables, herbs and greens, and crunchy toasted nuts or seeds, and toss with a bright vinaigrette. Still going? Add a poached egg or some sliced chicken.

Preheat oven to 450°. Cook black rice and wild rice in a large pot of boiling salted water until tender, 35–40 minutes; drain and rinse, shaking off as much water as possible. Spread out on a rimmed baking sheet and let cool.

Meanwhile, toss squash with ¼ cup oil on another baking sheet; season with salt and pepper. Roast, tossing once, until golden brown and tender, 20–25 minutes; let cool.

Whisk vinegar, honey, and remaining ¼ cup oil in a large bowl. Add black rice and wild rice, squash, scallions, pomegranate seeds, microgreens, and pistachios; season with salt and pepper and toss to combine.

DO AHEAD: Salad (without microgreens) can be made 4 hours ahead. Cover and chill.

Fresh herbs, such as parsley and cilantro, can be subbed for the microgreens, and any type of brown rice (short- or long-grain or basmati) can be used in place of the black rice. Look for antioxidant-rich black rice at Whole Foods.

APPLE CIDER-COOKED FARRO SALAD

4 SERVINGS

1 bay leaf

2 cups apple cider

Kosher salt

1 cup semi-pearled farro

2 Tbsp. apple cider vinegar

2 Tbsp. olive oil

Freshly ground black pepper

½ small celery root (celeriac), peeled, cut into matchsticks

½ medium sweet-tart apple, cored, cut into matchsticks

¼ small red onion, thinly sliced

½ cup fresh parsley leaves with tender stems

¼ cup coarsely chopped black olives

1 oz. Pecorino, shaved

Boiling farro in apple cider—a move we picked up from New York restaurant Charlie Bird—infuses grains with character. Try barley, rye berries, or brown rice, too.

Combine bay leaf, apple cider, and 2 cups water in a medium saucepan; season with salt. Bring to a boil, reduce heat to medium-high, and add farro. Simmer until al dente, 25–30 minutes; drain. Spread out on a rimmed baking sheet; let cool.

Toss farro, vinegar, and oil in a large bowl; season with salt and pepper. Add celery root, apple, onion, parsley, olives, and Pecorino and toss to combine; season with salt and pepper.

Farro, a hardy wheat kernel, is great in salads and soups, or use it in place of arborio rice to make farroto.

BARLEY, FENNEL, and BEET SALAD

6 SERVINGS

2 cups cooked barley (from about ⅔ cup dried)

1 fennel bulb, thinly sliced

2 small golden beets, thinly sliced

½ small red onion, thinly sliced

¼ cup chopped toasted almonds

¼ cup torn fresh mint

¼ cup olive oil

3 Tbsp. Sherry vinegar or red wine vinegar

Kosher salt and freshly ground black pepper

Our go-to grain salad is paired with crunchy fresh vegetables and brightened with mint (surprise!). Don't have barley? Try farro, freekeh, Israeli couscous, or our new favorite, red rice.

Toss barley, fennel bulb, beets, red onion, almonds, and mint in a large bowl with oil and vinegar; season with salt and pepper.

BEAN SALAD with LEMON and HERBS

6 SERVINGS

2 cups fresh cooked shell beans (such as cannellini or cranberry) or one 14-oz. can cannellini beans or chickpeas, rinsed

6 oz. green beans, trimmed, cut into 1" pieces

¼ cup fresh parsley leaves with tender stems

¼ cup olive oil

3 Tbsp. fresh chives, chopped

2 Tbsp. capers, chopped

1 Tbsp. finely grated lemon zest

2 Tbsp. fresh lemon juice

½ tsp. Aleppo pepper or ¼ tsp. crushed red pepper flakes

Kosher salt and freshly ground black pepper

Potlucks, we're ready! This herbaceous, protein-rich salad takes advantage of summer's fleeting fresh shell bean season. If you missed your window (or don't have time to shell), canned beans are fine—just be sure to rinse them.

Toss shell beans, green beans, parsley, oil, chives, capers, lemon zest, lemon juice, and Aleppo pepper in a large bowl; season with salt and pepper.

CRISPY BROWN RICE "KABBOULEH"

4 SERVINGS

2 Tbsp. dried currants

2 Tbsp. distilled white vinegar

¾ cup short-grain brown rice

Kosher salt

Vegetable oil (for frying; about 2 cups)

1½ cups coarsely chopped cauliflower florets

½ small bunch curly kale, ribs and stems removed, leaves coarsely chopped (about 2 cups)

½ small English hothouse cucumber, finely chopped

1 scallion, thinly sliced

⅓ cup olive oil

2 tsp. Aleppo pepper or ½ tsp. crushed red pepper flakes

2 tsp. sumac (optional)

Freshly ground black pepper

SPECIAL EQUIPMENT: A deep-fry thermometer

Is it crazy to cook rice, dry it out, and then deep-fry it? Maybe a little bit. But when you taste Jessica Koslow's unique and addictively crunchy twist on tabbouleh—served at her wildly popular L.A. restaurant, Sqirl—you'll appreciate the effort.

Combine currants and vinegar in a small bowl; let sit at least 2 hours and up to 1 day.

Cook rice in a large saucepan of boiling salted water until tender, 45–50 minutes. Drain rice, return to pot, cover, and let sit 10 minutes. Spread out on a baking sheet; let dry out overnight in an unlit oven or on countertop.

Fit a medium saucepan with thermometer and pour in vegetable oil to measure 2". Heat over medium-high heat until thermometer registers 350°. Working in 4 batches, cook rice until golden and puffed, about 1 minute. Using a fine-mesh sieve, transfer puffed rice to paper towels to drain; season with salt and let cool.

Meanwhile, pulse cauliflower in a food processor until finely chopped. Transfer to a large bowl. Working in batches, pulse kale in a food processor until finely chopped (be careful not to turn into a purée), adding to cauliflower as you go. Add puffed rice, currants with soaking liquid, cucumber, scallion, olive oil, Aleppo pepper, and sumac, if using; toss to combine and season with salt, black pepper, and more vinegar, if desired. **DO AHEAD:** Rice can be fried 5 days ahead. Store airtight at room temperature.

THE RESTAURANT BEHIND THE RECIPE

Sqirl

In the beginning, there was toast. Specifically, slices of burnt brioche, topped with homemade ricotta and spread to the very edges with small-batch jam in flavors like strawberry-rose geranium. And with that, Jessica Koslow turned a year's kitchen experience (followed by a three-year stint as a producer for *American Idol*) into Sqirl. What began in 2011 as an upstart preserves operation quickly spawned a sliver of a café serving breakfast and lunch in Silver Lake, Los Angeles's neighborhood du jour. Suddenly, people were waiting 20 minutes for that toast—in carbophobic L.A.!—forming a literal breadline to the tiny storefront.

And they kept coming back for dishes that, at the time, didn't exactly come off as crowd-pleasers on paper: a brown-rice bowl with sorrel pesto and preserved Meyer lemon; Danish rye topped with chicken and favas; and "Kabbouleh," the vegetal equivalent of a viral video. But Koslow's dishes managed to galvanize the very narrow crossover of food writers and L.A. salad obsessives. Turns out that in her hands, breakfast and lunch are what people want to eat all day long.

So, why no dinner service? "Breakfast is the natural progression of the jam," explains Koslow, who also saw an opportunity to bring "an expertise and desire for experimentation into meals that don't necessarily have it." For her bravery to go beyond eggs Benedict, she received four stars from *LA Weekly*.

Koslow and chef de cuisine Ria Dolly Barbosa Wilson might take something that she refers to as "grandma-traditional," like ricotta cavatelli, execute it perfectly, and then elevate it to the realm of greatness by, say, grating cured emu egg yolk on top. It's a high-low mix she likens to wearing H&M with an Hermès watch.

2

meat & poultry

SHORT RIB POT PIE

8 SERVINGS

CRUST

3 cups all-purpose flour

2 tsp. kosher salt

½ cup (1 stick) chilled unsalted butter, cut into pieces

½ cup vegetable shortening or beef lard

FILLING AND ASSEMBLY

3 lb. boneless beef short ribs, cut into 2" pieces

Kosher salt, freshly ground black pepper

½ cup all-purpose flour, plus more

2 Tbsp. olive oil

1 10-oz. package frozen pearl onions, thawed

4 garlic cloves, chopped

2 Tbsp. tomato paste

2 cups dry red wine

2 sprigs rosemary

6 sprigs thyme, plus 2 Tbsp. chopped thyme

Flaky sea salt (such as Maldon)

Heavy cream (for brushing)

Shortening is the secret to extra-flaky pie crust, but nothing compares to the flavor of butter in this rich and cozy dish. Use both, and you're golden.

CRUST

Pulse flour and salt in a food processor; add butter and shortening and pulse until mixture resembles coarse meal with a few pea-size pieces of butter remaining. Transfer flour mixture to a large bowl and drizzle with ½ cup ice water. Mix with a fork until dough just comes together.

Knead dough lightly, adding more water by the tablespoonful if needed, until no dry spots remain (dough will be slightly shaggy but moist). Form into a disk and wrap tightly in plastic. Chill until firm, at least 2 hours.
DO AHEAD: Crust can be made 2 days ahead; keep chilled.

FILLING AND ASSEMBLY

Preheat oven to 375°. Season short ribs with kosher salt and pepper; toss with ½ cup flour on a rimmed baking sheet. Heat oil in a large heavy pot over medium-high heat and, working in batches, shake excess flour from ribs and cook, turning occasionally, until deeply browned, 8–10 minutes per batch. Using a slotted spoon, transfer to a large bowl.

Add onions to same pot and cook, stirring occasionally, until golden brown; season with kosher salt and pepper and, using a slotted spoon, transfer to a small bowl. Reduce heat to medium, add garlic to pot, and cook, stirring, until softened, about 2 minutes. Add tomato paste and cook, stirring often, until slightly darkened in color, 5–8 minutes. Add wine, rosemary, and thyme sprigs, bring to a boil, and cook, scraping up browned bits, until liquid is reduced by half, 8–10 minutes. Add 6 cups water to pot and bring to a boil.

Return short ribs to pot; season with kosher salt and pepper. Reduce heat and simmer gently, uncovered, until short ribs are almost falling apart and liquid is thick enough to lightly coat a spoon, 2½–3 hours. Add onions and chopped thyme to pot and stir to break up short ribs; season filling with kosher salt and pepper. Remove herb sprigs.

Roll out dough on a lightly floured surface to about ⅛" thick. Transfer filling to a shallow 2-qt. baking dish. Place over filling and trim, leaving overhang. Tuck edges under and crimp. Cut a few slits in crust. Brush with cream and sprinkle with sea salt. Place dish on a rimmed baking sheet and bake until filling is bubbling and crust is golden brown, 50–60 minutes. Let sit 5–10 minutes before serving. **DO AHEAD:** Filling can be made 2 days ahead. Let cool; cover and chill. Reheat gently before assembling pie.

BOBBY'S CRUNCH BURGER

4 SERVINGS

COLESLAW

½ cup mayonnaise

1 Tbsp. apple cider vinegar

1 Tbsp. finely grated
   yellow onion

2 tsp. sugar

½ tsp. celery seeds

   Kosher salt and freshly
   ground black pepper

½ small head green cabbage,
   very thinly sliced

1 small carrot, peeled,
   coarsely grated

CHIPOTLE KETCHUP

½ cup ketchup

1 Tbsp. finely chopped canned
   chipotle chiles in adobo

   Kosher salt and freshly ground
   black pepper

BURGERS AND ASSEMBLY

1½ lb. ground beef chuck
   (20% fat)

   Kosher salt and freshly ground
   black pepper

2 Tbsp. vegetable oil

8 slices American cheese

4 soft sesame seed buns,
   split, toasted

   Sliced red onion, sliced
   pickled jalapeños, and thin
   potato chips (for serving)

According to Bobby Flay, every dish should have tons of flavors and a contrast of textures: crunchy, crispy, and crusty. Well, his burger has it all. From coleslaw to potato chips to burger and cheese, it's a full cookout on a (squishy-soft) bun.

COLESLAW

Whisk mayonnaise, vinegar, onion, sugar, and celery seeds in a large bowl; season with salt and pepper. Add cabbage and carrot and toss to coat; season with salt and pepper. Cover and chill at least 30 minutes. **DO AHEAD:** Coleslaw can be made 1 day ahead. Keep chilled.

CHIPOTLE KETCHUP

Whisk ketchup and chipotle chiles in a small bowl; season with salt and pepper. Cover and chill. **DO AHEAD:** Ketchup can be mixed 1 day ahead. Cover and chill.

BURGERS AND ASSEMBLY

Form meat into four 4"-diameter, ¾"-thick patties. Using your thumb, make an indentation in the center of each patty to help keep them flat as they cook. Season generously with salt and pepper.

Heat a large skillet, preferably cast iron, over medium-high heat, then heat oil in pan until smoking. Cook burgers until a deep brown crust has formed, about 2 minutes per side. Add 2 Tbsp. water to skillet, immediately cover skillet (hot oil will splatter), and cook to medium-rare, about 1 minute.

Uncover skillet and top each burger with 2 slices cheese. Add another 2 Tbsp. water to skillet; cover skillet and cook until cheese is melted and burgers are cooked to medium, about 1 minute longer.

Serve burgers on buns with chipotle ketchup, coleslaw, onion, jalapeños, and potato chips. **DO AHEAD:** Patties can be formed 4 hours ahead. Cover and chill.

"It's not so much about what cut of beef you use, it's about fat content," says Flay. "You want 20 percent; any less and it'll be too dry."

BISTRO STEAK
with BUTTERMILK
ONION RINGS

4 SERVINGS

VINAIGRETTE, STEAK, AND SAUCE

2 Tbsp. hazelnut, walnut,
  or olive oil

2 Tbsp. Sherry vinegar, divided

  Kosher salt, freshly ground
  black pepper

2 Tbsp. vegetable oil

1 1½-lb. hanger steak, center
  membrane removed, cut into
  4 equal pieces

2 Tbsp. unsalted butter

1 medium shallot, finely chopped

1 Tbsp. finely chopped fresh
  thyme

2 tsp. black peppercorns,
  coarsely chopped

2 tsp. dry green peppercorns,
  coarsely chopped

1 Tbsp. Dijon mustard

ONION RINGS AND ASSEMBLY

  Vegetable oil (for frying;
  about 3½ cups)

¾ cup buttermilk

2 Tbsp. apple cider vinegar

1½ cups all-purpose flour

  Kosher salt, freshly ground
  pepper

1 large onion, sliced ⅛" thick,
  rings separated

6 cups watercress leaves
  with tender stems

SPECIAL EQUIPMENT: A deep-fry
thermometer

Here's how to time this Franco-American feast: Have the salad and
onion ring components ready before you cook the steak and the
sauce, then keep the sauce warm while you fry the onions. Toss the
salad at the last moment—then open the wine!

VINAIGRETTE, STEAK, AND SAUCE

Whisk hazelnut oil and 1 Tbsp. vinegar in a small bowl; season with salt
and pepper. Set vinaigrette aside.

Heat vegetable oil in a large skillet over medium-high heat. Season steak
with salt and pepper and cook 6–8 minutes per side for medium-rare.
Let rest 10 minutes.

While steak rests, cook butter and shallot in same skillet over medium
heat, stirring occasionally, until shallot is softened and starting to brown,
about 4 minutes. Add thyme and peppercorns. Cook, stirring occasionally,
until mixture is fragrant, about 2 minutes. Add remaining 1 Tbsp. vinegar
and ½ cup water and simmer until flavors meld and sauce is thick enough
to coat a spoon, about 2 minutes. Remove sauce from heat and whisk in
mustard; season with salt and pepper. Keep warm.

ONION RINGS AND ASSEMBLY

Fit a medium saucepan with thermometer; pour in oil to measure 3".
Heat over medium-high heat until thermometer registers 350°.

Meanwhile, mix buttermilk and vinegar in a shallow bowl. Place flour
in another bowl or baking dish; season with salt and pepper. Toss onion
rings in flour mixture, shaking off excess, and transfer to a wire rack.
Working in batches, dip in buttermilk mixture, letting excess drip back
into bowl; toss again in flour.

Working in 2 or 3 batches and maintaining temperature of oil, fry onion
rings until golden brown and crisp, about 3 minutes per batch. Let drain
on paper towels; season with salt.

Toss watercress with reserved vinaigrette. Thinly slice steak against the
grain. Serve steak with sauce, watercress, and onion rings.

SKIRT STEAK FAJITAS
with GRILLED CABBAGE and SCALLIONS

8 SERVINGS

These smoky fajitas are a Tex-Mex take on *carne asada* tacos, with a surprising vegetal twist. According to chef Josef Centeno of L.A.'s Bar Amá, the vegetables should still have plenty of bite when you pull them off the grill. Serve with spicy chile sauce.

DRIED CHILE SALSA

1½ oz. dried chiles de árbol

1½ oz. ancho chiles

1 medium white onion, chopped

4 garlic cloves, peeled

1 Tbsp. kosher salt

⅓ cup distilled white vinegar

STEAK

4 garlic cloves, peeled

¼ cup fresh lime juice

¼ cup olive oil

3 Tbsp. hot smoked Spanish paprika

2 Tbsp. chopped fresh cilantro

1 Tbsp. ground cumin

1 tsp. kosher salt

1 tsp. onion powder

2 lb. skirt steak, cut into 4 equal pieces

VEGETABLES AND ASSEMBLY

½ medium head green cabbage, cut into 2 wedges, core intact

1 large white onion, halved with some root end attached

1 bunch scallions, trimmed

6 Tbsp. olive oil, divided

Kosher salt, freshly ground black pepper

¼ small red onion, finely chopped

3 Tbsp. fresh lime juice

1 Tbsp. chopped fresh cilantro

Warm flour tortillas (for serving)

DRIED CHILE SALSA

Toast chiles in a dry medium skillet over high heat, turning often, until fragrant, about 3 minutes. Let cool slightly, then remove stems and seeds. Place chiles, onion, garlic, salt, and 1½ cups water in a medium saucepan. Bring to a boil. Reduce heat and simmer until very soft, 15–20 minutes. Purée chile mixture in a blender until smooth. Strain into a medium bowl and mix in vinegar. **DO AHEAD:** Salsa can be made 4 days ahead. Cover and chill.

STEAK

Purée garlic, lime juice, oil, paprika, cilantro, cumin, salt, and onion powder in a blender until smooth. Transfer marinade to a resealable plastic bag and add steak. Seal bag and turn to coat; chill at least 4 hours. **DO AHEAD:** Steak can be marinated 1 day ahead. Keep chilled.

VEGETABLES AND ASSEMBLY

Prepare grill for medium-high heat. (Alternatively, heat a grill pan over medium-high heat.) Drizzle cabbage, white onion, and scallions with 4 Tbsp. oil; season with salt and pepper. Grill, turning occasionally, until vegetables are charred and softened, about 4 minutes for scallions, 10–12 minutes for cabbage and onion. Let vegetables cool slightly.

Core cabbage and cut into bite-size pieces along with scallions and onion. Toss chopped vegetables in a large bowl with red onion, lime juice, cilantro, and remaining 2 Tbsp. oil; season with salt and pepper.

Remove steak from marinade, scraping off excess; season with salt and pepper. Grill steak until medium-rare, about 3 minutes per side. Transfer to a cutting board and let rest 5–10 minutes before slicing. Serve steak with vegetables, tortillas, and dried chile salsa.

SOY and SESAME
SHORT RIBS

4 SERVINGS

½ apple (skin on), cored, chopped

6 garlic cloves, peeled, crushed

½ cup orange marmalade

2 Tbsp. light brown sugar

2 Tbsp. toasted sesame oil

2 Tbsp. toasted sesame seeds

1 Tbsp. dry sake or dry white wine

2 tsp. gochugaru (Korean red
   pepper powder)

1½ tsp. freshly ground black
   pepper

½ cup soy sauce

2 lb. ¼"-thick cross-cut bone-in
   beef short ribs (flanken style)

   Vegetable oil (for grilling)

Takashi Inoue—the owner of Takashi, a Korean-inspired tabletop grilling restaurant in New York City—loves to use this marinade on any cut of beef (try hanger), chicken wings, or pork ribs.

Pulse apple, garlic, marmalade, brown sugar, sesame oil, sesame seeds, sake, gochugaru, and pepper in a food processor or blender until garlic and apple are finely chopped.

Transfer to a large dish and mix in soy sauce. Add ribs and turn to coat. Let sit, massaging meat and turning occasionally, at least 10 minutes.

Prepare grill for medium-high heat; oil grate with vegetable oil. Remove ribs from marinade and grill, turning once, until lightly charred and cooked through, about 2 minutes per side for medium-rare.

DO AHEAD: Meat can be marinated 1 hour ahead. Chill.

Flanken-style short ribs have been thinly cut across the bone rather than parallel to it (that's English-style). When they're marinated and grilled, the result is chewy and super-flavorful. You might find flanken-cut ribs at your butcher, but you're often better off ordering ahead. Your best bet? Visit an Asian grocery store.

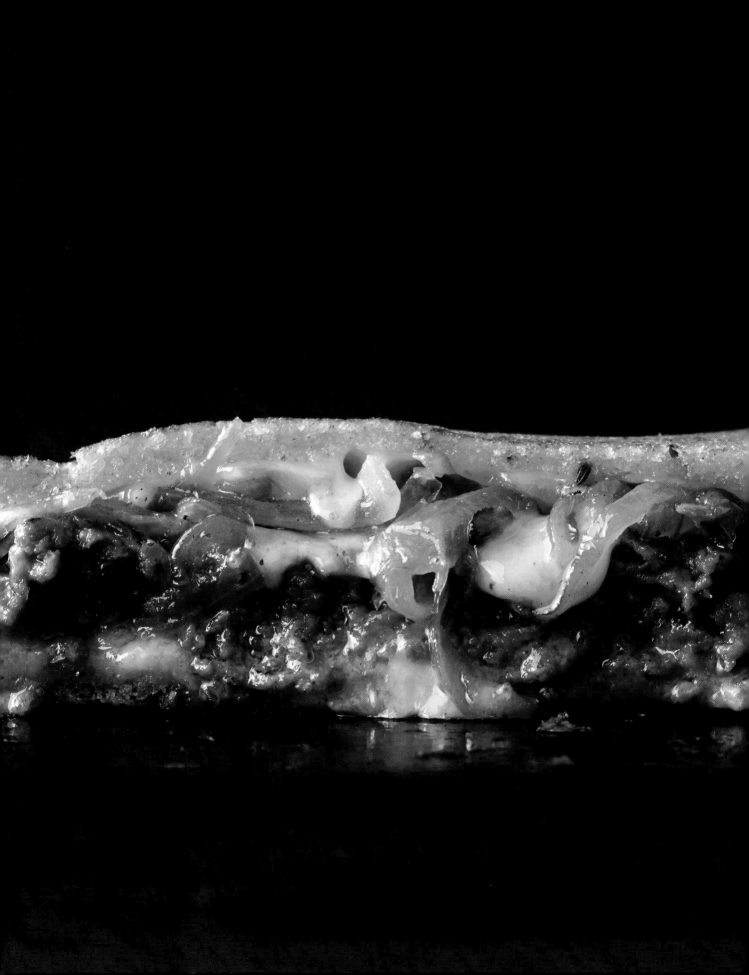

The ULTIMATE PATTY MELT

MAKES 4

CARAMELIZED ONIONS

2 Tbsp. vegetable oil

2 large onions, thinly sliced

PATTIES AND ASSEMBLY

¼ small onion, finely chopped

1 lb. ground beef chuck (20% fat)

1 Tbsp. ketchup

½ tsp. garlic powder

1 tsp. kosher salt

¼ tsp. freshly ground black pepper

1 Tbsp. vegetable oil

8 slices seeded rye bread
   (preferably Levy's)

4 oz. aged sharp cheddar,
   thinly sliced

4 oz. Swiss cheese (such as
   Emmenthal), thinly sliced

8 tsp. mayonnaise

Seasoned ground-beef patties, caramelized onions, and melty cheese (two kinds!)—chefs are learning what diner fans already know: A patty melt is griddled, gooey genius. Here's how to get it at home.

CARAMELIZED ONIONS

Heat oil in a medium skillet over medium heat and cook onions, stirring often and adding water as needed to prevent burning, until deep golden brown and very soft, 20–25 minutes. Set aside.

PATTIES AND ASSEMBLY

Gently mix onion, beef, ketchup, garlic powder, salt, and pepper in a medium bowl. Divide into 4 portions and press each between 2 pieces of parchment or waxed paper until about ¼" thick (you want them roughly the same dimensions as the bread you're using).

Heat oil in a large skillet, preferably cast iron, over medium-high heat. Working in 2 batches, cook patties, pressing gently, until browned but still pink in the center, about 2 minutes per side. Transfer to a plate.

Wipe out skillet and reduce heat to medium. Top 4 slices of bread with cheddar, then beef patties, caramelized onions, and Swiss cheese. Close up sandwiches and spread each top with 1 tsp. mayonnaise. Place in pan, mayonnaise side down, and weight with a foil-covered heavy pan. Cook until bottom slice is golden brown, about 3 minutes. Remove weighted pan and spread the top of each sandwich with 1 tsp. mayonnaise. Flip and weight again. Cook until other side is golden brown and cheese is melted, about 3 minutes.

DO AHEAD: Patties can be formed 8 hours ahead. Cover and chill.

A swipe of mayo, not butter, on the outside of the bread encourages that gorgeous griddled exterior. Weigh down the sandwich with a heavy pan to compress the elements for a toasty, melty sandwich that stays put.

HORSERADISH-and-PARSLEY-STUFFED RIB-EYE ROAST

8 SERVINGS

8 anchovy fillets packed in oil, drained, finely chopped

4 garlic cloves, finely grated

1 cup finely chopped fresh parsley

⅓ cup grated horseradish

⅓ cup olive oil

2 tsp. crushed red pepper flakes

½ tsp. freshly grated nutmeg

Kosher salt, freshly ground black pepper

1 4–5-lb. boneless beef rib-eye roast

The rib-eye roast comes from the same area as the standing rib roast, but it's a more manageable size (and cooks more evenly). It has all the fat—a.k.a. flavor—of prime rib. Ask your butcher for the bones and roast them with the meat.

Combine anchovies, garlic, parsley, horseradish, oil, red pepper flakes, and nutmeg in a small bowl; season with salt and pepper. Set 2 Tbsp. of mixture aside.

Place rib-eye roast, fat side down, on a cutting board with a short end toward you. Holding a sharp slicing knife about 1" above cutting board, make a shallow cut along the entire length of a long side of roast. Continue cutting deeper into the roast, lifting and unfurling meat with your free hand, until it can lie flat. Season both sides with salt and pepper.

Spread parsley mixture over roast and roll up so fat cap is on top; tie at 1" intervals with kitchen twine. Rub outside of roast with reserved parsley mixture and wrap tightly in plastic wrap. Chill at least 8 hours and up to 1 day.

Let roast sit at room temperature 1 hour to help it roast evenly.

Preheat oven to 400°. Place meat on a rack set inside a roasting pan and roast, rotating once, until fat is golden brown and starting to render, 40–50 minutes.

Reduce temperature to 300° and continue to roast until an instant-read thermometer inserted into the thickest part registers 125° for medium-rare, 1–1½ hours longer. Transfer to a cutting board; let rest at least 30 minutes before slicing.

For a step-by-step primer on how to butterfly your roast, go to bonappetit.com/butterfly. Or ask your butcher to do it for you.

PORK and SQUASH STEW with CHILES

6 SERVINGS

- 3 lb. boneless pork shoulder (Boston butt), cut into 2" pieces
- 1 Tbsp. ground coriander
- 10 garlic cloves, finely chopped, divided
- 1 Tbsp. kosher salt, plus more
  Freshly ground black pepper
- ½ cup raw shelled pumpkin seeds
- 6 dried New Mexico or guajillo chiles
- 2 chiles de árbol or ½ tsp. crushed red pepper flakes
- 2 large yellow onions, cut into ⅛"-thick wedges, divided
- 2 Tbsp. vegetable oil
- 4 sprigs oregano
- ½ kabocha squash (about 1 lb.), peeled, seeds removed, cut into 1" pieces
- 1 delicata squash, seeds removed, cut into ½"-thick slices
- ½ small red onion, thinly sliced
- ¼ cup fresh lime juice
  Cilantro sprigs (for serving)

This stew calls for water instead of stock. It will be plenty flavorful, though: The pork shoulder will create a rich cooking liquid on its own.

Combine pork, coriander, half of garlic, and 1 Tbsp. salt in a large bowl; season with pepper and toss. Cover; chill at least 4 hours.

Preheat oven to 350°. Toast pumpkin seeds on a rimmed baking sheet, tossing occasionally, until golden, about 5 minutes; set aside.

Toast chiles on clean baking sheet until slightly darkened, about 5 minutes. Let cool slightly, then remove stems, and seeds, if you prefer less heat. Place chiles, half of yellow onion, remaining garlic, and 1 cup hot water in a blender; let sit 10 minutes to soften chiles. Blend until smooth; set chile purée aside.

Heat oil in a large Dutch oven over medium-high heat. Working in batches, cook pork, turning occasionally, until browned, 8–10 minutes; transfer to a plate.

Pour off fat from pot. Cook chile purée in pot over medium-high heat, stirring occasionally, until reduced by half, 8–10 minutes. Add pork, oregano, remaining yellow onion, and 10 cups water to pot; season with salt and pepper. Bring to a boil, reduce heat, and simmer, partially covered, skimming occasionally, until pork is very tender, 3–3½ hours.

Add squash to stew and cook, uncovered, until pork is falling apart and squash is soft, 30–35 minutes; season with salt and pepper.

Toss red onion and lime juice in a small bowl; let sit, tossing occasionally, 30 minutes.

Serve stew with red onion, cilantro, and reserved pumpkin seeds.

DO AHEAD: Pork can be marinated 2 days ahead; keep chilled. Stew can be made 3 days ahead; let cool, then cover and chill.

GOCHUJANG PORK SHOULDER STEAKS

4 SERVINGS

8 garlic cloves, peeled, crushed

1 2" piece ginger, peeled, sliced

½ cup dry sake

½ cup gochujang (Korean hot pepper paste)

½ cup mirin (sweet Japanese rice wine)

¼ cup vegetable oil, plus more for grilling

1½ lb. skinless, boneless pork shoulder (Boston butt), sliced ¾" thick

In this Korean-inspired recipe from chef Rachel Yang of Seattle's Trove and Joule, the fermented chile paste *gochujang* gives the pork a burnished red color and hints at its spiciness. It's available at hmart.com.

Purée garlic, ginger, sake, gochujang, mirin, and ¼ cup oil in a blender. Set ¼ cup marinade aside; chill. Transfer remaining marinade to a large dish. Add pork; turn to coat. Chill, turning occasionally, at least 2 hours.

Prepare grill for medium-high heat; oil grate. Remove pork from marinade and grill, basting with reserved marinade, turning occasionally, and moving pork to a cooler area if flare-up occurs, until cooked to desired doneness, 8–10 minutes for medium-rare.

Transfer pork to a cutting board and let rest 5 minutes before thinly slicing against the grain.

DO AHEAD: Pork can be marinated 1 day ahead. Keep chilled.

Keep an eye on the edge of the meat where it touches the grill: When it's browned, turn the pork over.

VIETNAMESE PORK
CHOPS WITH
PICKLED WATERMELON
P. 84

opposite:
BRAISED SPICED
PORK WITH
CAO LAU NOODLES
P. 85

VIETNAMESE PORK CHOPS
with PICKLED WATERMELON

8 SERVINGS

PICKLED WATERMELON RIND

4 lb. watermelon

1 serrano chile, thinly sliced, seeds removed if desired

1 1" piece peeled ginger, thinly sliced

2 star anise pods

4 tsp. kosher salt

1 tsp. black peppercorns

1 cup sugar

1 cup unseasoned rice vinegar

PORK CHOPS

2 small shallots, thinly sliced into rings

¼ cup reduced-sodium soy sauce

2 Tbsp. fish sauce (such as nam pla or nuoc nam)

2 Tbsp. sugar

½ tsp. Sriracha

4 1"-thick bone-in pork chops (about 2½ lb. total)

SALAD

6 Tbsp. vegetable oil, divided

4 small shallots, thinly sliced

Kosher salt

1 Tbsp. unseasoned rice vinegar

1 tsp. reduced-sodium soy sauce

¼ tsp. sugar

Freshly ground black pepper

4 cups trimmed purslane or arugula

½ lb. seedless watermelon, rind removed, cut into pieces, thinly sliced

½ cup Pickled Watermelon Rind, thinly sliced

A bold mix of salty, sweet, and acidic components. Crunchy slabs of melon and sharp greens keep it fresh; meaty chops provide depth. Be sure to pickle the watermelon a day ahead.

PICKLED WATERMELON RIND

Using a vegetable peeler, remove tough green rind from watermelon; discard. Slice watermelon 1" thick. Cut away all but ¼" flesh from each slice; reserve ½ lb. for salad. Cut rind into 1" pieces. (You should have about 4 cups.)

Bring chile, ginger, star anise, salt, peppercorns, sugar, vinegar, and ½ cup water to a boil in a large saucepan, stirring to dissolve sugar and salt. Add watermelon rind and return to a boil; reduce heat and simmer until just tender, about 5 minutes. Remove from heat and let cool, setting a small lid or plate directly on top of rind to keep submerged in brine, if needed.

Transfer rind and liquid to an airtight container; cover and chill at least 12 hours. Makes 1 quart.

PORK CHOPS

Whisk shallots, soy sauce, fish sauce, sugar, and Sriracha in a shallow baking dish. Add pork chops and turn to coat. Cover and chill, turning occasionally, at least 1 hour.

Prepare grill for medium-high heat. Remove pork chops from marinade, scraping off excess, and grill until cooked through, about 3 minutes per side.

DO AHEAD: Pork chops can be marinated 12 hours ahead. Keep chilled.

SALAD

Heat 4 Tbsp. oil in a small saucepan over medium heat. Add shallots and cook, stirring occasionally, until golden brown and crisp, about 4 minutes. Transfer to paper towels to drain; season with salt.

Whisk vinegar, soy sauce, sugar, and remaining 2 Tbsp. oil in a large bowl; season with salt and pepper. Add purslane, reserved watermelon, and pickled watermelon rind; season with salt and pepper and toss gently to coat.

Serve pork chops with watermelon salad topped with fried shallots.

BRAISED SPICED PORK
with CAO LAU NOODLES

6 SERVINGS

PORK

2 medium shallots, finely chopped

2 lemongrass stalks, tough outer layer removed, stalks lightly smashed, finely chopped

2 Tbsp. reduced-sodium soy sauce

1 Tbsp. fish sauce

1 Tbsp. hot chili paste (such as sambal oelek)

2 tsp. kosher salt

2 tsp. sugar

1½ tsp. Chinese five-spice powder

1 lb. boneless pork shoulder (Boston butt), halved

1 lb. skin-on pork belly, halved

2 Tbsp. vegetable oil

6 garlic cloves, finely chopped

NOODLES AND ASSEMBLY

½ cup plus 1 Tbsp. vegetable oil

4 wonton or egg roll wrappers, cut into 4 squares

Kosher salt

1 lb. dried wide rice noodles

8 oz. mung bean sprouts (about 2 cups)

1 Fresno chile, with seeds, sliced

1 lime, cut into wedges

Mixed fresh tender herbs (such as mint, cilantro, and Thai basil), hot chili paste (such as sambal oelek; for serving)

This traditional Vietnamese recipe, interpreted by David Tanis, is the perfect synthesis of fresh and long-cooked textures; rich, sweet, and herbal flavors; and juicy and crunchy garnishes. Serve with extra herbs, chiles, and lime so everyone can customize his or her own bowl.

PORK

Combine shallots, lemongrass, soy sauce, fish sauce, chili paste, salt, sugar, and five-spice powder in a large bowl. Add pork shoulder and pork belly and toss to coat. Cover and chill at least 3 hours.

Remove pork from marinade, scraping excess back into bowl; set marinade aside. Heat oil in a large Dutch oven or other heavy pot over medium-high heat. Cook pork, turning occasionally, until browned all over, 10–15 minutes; transfer to a plate.

Pour off all but 1 Tbsp. fat from pot. Add garlic and cook, stirring, until fragrant but without taking on any color, about 1 minute. Add reserved marinade and 4 cups water and bring to a boil. Add pork, reduce heat, and simmer, partially covered, turning pork occasionally, until fork-tender but not falling apart, 1–1½ hours. Let cool in liquid.

DO AHEAD: Pork can be braised 2 days ahead; cover and chill.

NOODLES AND ASSEMBLY

Heat ½ cup oil in a small skillet over medium-high heat. Working in batches, fry wonton wrappers until golden brown, about 30 seconds per side. Transfer to paper towels to drain; season with salt.

Cook noodles according to package directions. Using tongs or a spider, transfer noodles to a colander and run under cold water to stop cooking; transfer to a large bowl. Toss with remaining 1 Tbsp. oil; set aside. (Keep pot of boiling water handy for reheating noodles.)

Remove pork from braising liquid and slice ¼" thick. Bring braising liquid to a boil. Add ½ cup water. The flavor should still be intense and slightly salty; adjust with more water if needed. Simmer 2 minutes, remove from heat and add sliced pork. Let cool slightly.

Just before serving, return noodle cooking water to a boil. Place noodles in a fine-mesh sieve and lower into hot water to reheat, 30 seconds. Divide noodles among bowls. Place bean sprouts in sieve and cook in same pot of water 30 seconds; drain and place on top of noodles. Remove pork from cooking liquid and place on top of noodles. Ladle some cooking liquid over. Serve with chile, lime wedges, wontons, a handful of herbs, and a dab of chili paste.

MARMALADE-GLAZED HOLIDAY HAM

20 SERVINGS

½ cup bitter orange marmalade

¼ cup honey, pure maple syrup, or light brown sugar

1 Tbsp. adobo sauce, Aleppo pepper, or spicy Dijon mustard

3 Tbsp. bourbon, Cognac, or dark rum

1 12–14-lb. whole cured, smoked, bone-in ham

ACCOMPANIMENTS

Martin's potato rolls, Dijon mustard, cornichons

Forget about every canapé or thing-on-a-stick that you were planning to serve at your party. Forget about platters. All you need is a smoked bone-in ham. Order a good one (dartagnan.com is a fine choice), score, glaze, and bake it. Put that ham on a big wooden board, provide a blade with which to slice it (a carving knife, say), and a vehicle with which to devour it (we love Martin's potato rolls; order at potatorolls.com). Then watch your guests turn into a pack of wolves, leaving you with just a bone—perfect for tomorrow's split-pea soup— and the memory of the best holiday party ever.

Preheat oven to 350°. Whisk marmalade, honey, adobo, and bourbon in a medium bowl.

Place ham on a rack in a large roasting pan and add 2 cups water (this keeps drippings from scorching). Score fat in a crosshatch pattern, cutting about ½" deep.

Brush ham with glaze and roast, basting with pan juices every 20 minutes and tenting with foil if needed, until an instant-read thermometer inserted into the thickest part of ham registers 135°, 1½–2 hours.

Let rest 10 minutes or more before carving.

Amazing Glazes

A sweet-spicy glaze is an impressive—and easy—party trick. Use the formula here, choosing one of each from the sweet, spicy, and boozy columns.

THE BASE	SWEET	SPICY	BOOZY
½ CUP BITTER ORANGE MARMALADE	¼ CUP LIGHT BROWN SUGAR	1 TBSP. SPICY DIJON MUSTARD	3 TBSP. DARK RUM
	or	*or*	*or*
	HONEY	ADOBO SAUCE	COGNAC
	or	*or*	*or*
	PURE MAPLE SYRUP	ALEPPO PEPPER	BOURBON

SLOW-ROASTED PORK SHOULDER with MUSTARD and SAGE

8 SERVINGS

1 skinless, bone-in pork shoulder (Boston butt; 5–6 lb.)

Kosher salt, freshly ground black pepper

½ cup Dijon mustard

¼ cup finely chopped fresh sage

2 Tbsp. finely chopped fresh marjoram

4 garlic cloves, finely chopped

Serve this fork-tender pork over a bed of soft polenta for catching the juices, with a simply dressed salad on the side. Any leftovers will make for amazing sandwiches the next day.

Place a rack in lower third of oven; preheat to 325°. Season pork with salt and pepper. Mix mustard, sage, marjoram, and garlic in a small bowl. Spread all over pork, working it into all the crevices.

Place pork, fat side up, on a rack set inside a roasting pan and roast, basting with pan juices about every hour and tenting with foil if pork browns too quickly, until pork is well browned and very tender, 5–6 hours (depending on size of pork shoulder).

Let pork rest at least 10 minutes before serving (the meat should pull apart easily).

ROAST PORK TENDERLOIN
with CARROT ROMESCO

4 SERVINGS

¼ cup pine nuts

1½ lb. small carrots, peeled, halved lengthwise if larger

5 Tbsp. olive oil, divided

Kosher salt, freshly ground black pepper

1 large pork tenderloin (about 1½ lb.)

1 small garlic clove, finely grated

1 tsp. Aleppo pepper or ½ tsp. crushed red pepper flakes

2 Tbsp. red wine vinegar, divided

2 cups spicy greens (such as watercress or baby mustard)

Romesco is to Spain what pesto is to Italy. Typically made with red peppers, this carrot version sparked some new ideas. (See below.)

Preheat oven to 350°. Toast pine nuts on a rimmed baking sheet, tossing occasionally, until golden brown, 8–10 minutes; let cool.

Increase temperature to 450°. Toss carrots with 1 Tbsp. oil on another rimmed baking sheet; season with salt and black pepper. Roast, tossing occasionally, until softened and browned, 15–20 minutes; let cool slightly.

Meanwhile, heat 1 Tbsp. oil in a large ovenproof skillet over medium-high heat. Season pork with salt and black pepper and cook, turning occasionally, until golden brown, 10–15 minutes. Transfer skillet to oven and roast pork until a thermometer inserted into thickest portion registers 145°, 8–10 minutes. Let rest 5 minutes before slicing.

Pulse pine nuts, garlic, and remaining 3 Tbsp. oil in a food processor to a coarse paste. Add Aleppo pepper, one-fourth of carrots, 1 Tbsp. vinegar, and 1 Tbsp. water. Process, adding more water as needed, to a coarse purée; season romesco with salt, black pepper, and more vinegar, if desired.

Toss greens with remaining carrots and remaining 1 Tbsp. vinegar in a large bowl; season with salt and black pepper. Serve pork with romesco and salad.

BA'S SUPER SAUCE

Follow the directions for the carrot romesco, using these roasted vegetables and toasted nuts instead. Estimate ¼ cup nuts for every 1¼ cups cooked vegetables. You have our permission to improvise!

BEET + HAZELNUT
Spoon alongside roast cod or whole grilled trout.

BROCCOLI + ALMOND
Spread on a sandwich with sharp provolone cheese and wilted greens.

TOMATO + PECAN
Serve with a grilled steak or soft-cooked eggs.

POMEGRANATE-GLAZED
RACK of LAMB

8 SERVINGS

3 Tbsp. chopped fresh oregano

2 Tbsp. olive oil

3 Tbsp. plus 2 tsp. pomegranate molasses

3 Tbsp. fennel seeds, divided

Kosher salt, freshly ground black pepper

2 medium fennel bulbs, sliced lengthwise

1 small onion, thinly sliced

2 3–3½-lb. racks of lamb, rib bones frenched

2 Tbsp. vegetable oil

2 Tbsp. white wine vinegar

¼ cup pomegranate seeds

INGREDIENT INFO: Pomegranate molasses is available at Middle Eastern markets and some supermarkets, and online.

Two racks make enough for each person to have two chops. Cut between each bone individually for single chops, or cut into double-rib portions.

Preheat oven to 425°. Mix oregano, olive oil, 3 Tbsp. pomegranate molasses, and 2 Tbsp. fennel seeds in a small bowl; season oregano mixture with salt and pepper.

Toss fennel, onion, remaining 1 Tbsp. fennel seeds, and remaining 2 tsp. pomegranate molasses in a large baking dish or roasting pan; season with salt and pepper. Distribute evenly across bottom of pan.

Season lamb with salt and pepper. Heat 1 Tbsp. vegetable oil in a large skillet, preferably cast iron, over medium heat. Cook 1 rack of lamb, fat side down, until golden brown, 8–10 minutes. Turn and cook until other side is just browned, about 5 minutes. Transfer to dish with fennel mixture, placing fat side up, and rub with half of oregano mixture. Wipe out skillet and repeat with remaining 1 Tbsp. vegetable oil, second rack of lamb, and remaining oregano mixture.

Roast lamb and vegetables until an instant-read thermometer inserted into thickest part of lamb registers 125° for medium-rare, 25–30 minutes. Transfer lamb to a cutting board and let rest at least 10 minutes before carving.

Meanwhile, toss vegetables in pan drippings to coat and continue to roast until tender and starting to caramelize, 10–15 minutes. Remove from oven; add vinegar and toss to combine.

Serve lamb over vegetables topped with pomegranate seeds.

Be sure to ask for American lamb rather than New Zealand. The delicate New Zealand breeds are much smaller than the meaty domestic varieties, so the cooking time (and yield) would change significantly.

SPICED LAMB BURGER

8 SERVINGS

2½ lb. ground lamb, preferably shoulder

1 medium onion, very finely chopped

¾ cup chopped fresh flat-leaf parsley

1 Tbsp. ground coriander

¾ tsp. ground cumin

½ tsp. ground cinnamon

2 tsp. kosher salt

1½ tsp. freshly ground black pepper

¼ cup olive oil, plus more for grilling

8 thick medium pita breads with pockets

Thanks to Anissa Helou for one of our favorite new grilling recipes. As the ground lamb cooks inside the pita, the fat renders into the bread, creating a crunchy, compact, vibrantly flavored Moroccan meat pie that's unlike any burger you've ever had.

Using a fork, mix lamb, onion, parsley, coriander, cumin, cinnamon, salt, pepper, and ¼ cup oil in a large bowl. Cover and chill at least 1 hour.

Prepare grill for medium heat and oil grate. Working one at a time, open each pita pocket by cutting along seam, halfway around perimeter. Spoon filling into pitas, spreading to edges. Close, pressing on filling to seal.

Grill pitas until filling is cooked through and bread is crisp, about 5 minutes per side.

DO AHEAD: Filling can be made 8 hours ahead. Keep chilled. Pita breads can be stuffed 1 hour ahead; cover and chill.

GRILLED LEG of LAMB
with HERB SALT

HERB SALT

8 fresh sage leaves

¼ cup fresh rosemary leaves

2 Tbsp. fresh thyme leaves

1 cup kosher salt

1 Tbsp. crushed red pepper flakes

1 tsp. fennel seeds

¼ tsp. freshly ground black pepper

LAMB

4 lb. boneless leg of lamb

2 Tbsp. olive oil

ANCHOVY MAYONNAISE

1 large egg yolk

1 tsp. Dijon mustard

2 Tbsp. fresh lemon juice

½ cup grapeseed oil

¾ cup olive oil

6 anchovy fillets packed in oil, drained, very finely chopped

Kosher salt, freshly ground black pepper

For stress-free, no-sweat hosting, grill the lamb a few hours ahead of time and slice it at room temperature. Perfect for a summer dinner.

HERB SALT

Pulse sage, rosemary, and thyme in a food processor until coarsely chopped. Add salt, red pepper flakes, fennel seeds, and black pepper and pulse to blend.

DO AHEAD: Salt can be made 2 months ahead. Store airtight at room temperature.

LAMB

Cutting along seams where lamb leg naturally separates, portion into 4 large pieces, trimming any excess fat and sinew. Rub lamb with oil and herb salt. Let sit at room temperature 1 hour before grilling.

Prepare a grill for high heat. Grill lamb, turning often, until lightly charred and an instant-read thermometer registers 130°, 20–30 minutes. Transfer to a cutting board; let rest 10 minutes. While lamb sits, make anchovy mayonnaise (below). Thinly slice lamb against the grain and serve with anchovy mayonnaise.

DO AHEAD: Lamb can be seasoned 2 days ahead. Cover and chill.

ANCHOVY MAYONNAISE

Whisk egg yolk, mustard, and 1 tsp. lemon juice in a small bowl. Whisking constantly, gradually drizzle in grapeseed oil, then olive oil, drop by drop at first, until mayonnaise is thickened and smooth. Whisk in anchovies and remaining lemon juice; season with salt and pepper. Cover and chill.

DO AHEAD: Mayonnaise can be made 1 day ahead. Keep chilled.

MOROCCAN CHICKEN BROCHETTES

8 SERVINGS

GARLIC SAUCE

4 garlic cloves, finely chopped

  Kosher salt

⅓ cup olive oil

3 Tbsp. plain yogurt

CHICKEN

2 lb. skinless, boneless chicken thighs, cut into 2" pieces

2 garlic cloves, chopped

½ cup finely chopped fresh flat-leaf parsley

2 tsp. ground cumin

2 tsp. paprika

¼ tsp. crushed red pepper flakes

  Kosher salt

  Vegetable oil (for grilling)

  Warm pita bread, labneh (Lebanese strained yogurt), chopped tomatoes, and fresh mint leaves (for serving)

SPECIAL EQUIPMENT: Sixteen 8" bamboo or metal skewers

Anissa Helou, the author of *Levant: Recipes and Memories from the Middle East,* uses a dry spice rub to make these incredibly flavorful chicken kebabs crispy and juicy, too. She explains that it's believed that the liquid in a marinade can dilute the flavors of herbs and spices, but with a dry rub, the moisture from the meat is what draws them in.

GARLIC SAUCE

Place garlic in a mortar; season with salt and pound to a very fine paste. (Alternatively, place garlic on a cutting board, season with salt, and mash with the side of a chef's knife.) Transfer garlic paste to a small bowl and gradually whisk in oil.

Very gradually whisk yogurt into garlic mixture until emulsified. (Add too fast and sauce will break. If it does break, gradually whisk in 1 tsp. water just before serving.)

DO AHEAD: Garlic sauce can be made 6 hours ahead. Cover and chill.

CHICKEN

Toss chicken, garlic, parsley, cumin, paprika, and red pepper flakes in a medium bowl; season with salt. Cover and chill at least 2 hours.

Prepare grill for medium-high heat and oil grate. Thread chicken onto skewers. Grill, turning occasionally, until cooked through, 8–12 minutes. Serve with garlic sauce, pita bread, labneh, tomatoes, and mint.

DO AHEAD: Chicken can be marinated 12 hours ahead. Keep chilled.

Dark-meat chicken is the best for grilled skewers: Unlike lean breasts, boneless thighs have plenty of fat, so they won't dry out.

PAN-ROASTED
CHICKEN
with SHALLOTS

4 SERVINGS

2 garlic cloves, peeled

½ cup fresh mint leaves

2 Tbsp. olive oil

1 cup fresh flat-leaf parsley
   leaves, plus more for serving

1 tsp. kosher salt, plus more

¼ tsp. freshly ground black
   pepper, plus more

1 3½–4-lb. chicken, halved,
   breast bone removed

8 small shallots, peeled,
   root end trimmed

Rubbing the marinade onto only the flesh side puts it in direct contact with the meat and lets the skin get extra-crisp with no fear of burned bits in the skillet.

Pulse garlic, mint, oil, and 1 cup parsley in a food processor until very finely chopped; season with 1 tsp. salt and ¼ tsp. pepper.

Season chicken with salt and pepper and spread herb paste over flesh side. Place, skin side up, on a wire rack set inside a rimmed baking sheet; chill at least 3 hours (the dryer the skin, the crisper it'll get).

Place a rack in lower third of oven; preheat to 425°. Pat chicken dry and place, skin side down, in a large ovenproof skillet, preferably cast iron. Set over medium-high heat and cook, undisturbed, until skin is golden brown, about 5 minutes.

Add shallots to skillet and transfer to oven. Roast, turning shallots once, 20–25 minutes. Turn skin side up and roast until skin is very crisp and an instant-read thermometer inserted into the thickest part of thigh registers 160°, 8–10 minutes longer. Serve chicken with shallots, parsley, and any pan juices.

DO AHEAD: Chicken can be rubbed with herb paste 1 day ahead. Keep chilled.

CHICKEN and DUMPLINGS with MUSHROOMS

6 SERVINGS

CHICKEN STEW

- 6 oz. slab bacon, cut into ¼" pieces
- ¼ cup all-purpose flour
- 4 chicken legs (drumsticks with thighs; about 2 lb.)
- Kosher salt, freshly ground black pepper
- 1½ lb. mixed mushrooms
- 1 medium onion, chopped
- 6 garlic cloves, crushed
- ¼ cup dry white wine
- 6 sprigs thyme
- 2 bay leaves
- 8 cups low-sodium chicken broth

DUMPLINGS AND ASSEMBLY

- ¾ tsp. kosher salt, plus more
- 1 cup all-purpose flour
- 2 tsp. baking powder
- ½ tsp. freshly grated nutmeg
- ⅛ tsp. freshly ground black pepper
- 2 large eggs
- ¼ cup whole milk

There's a lot to love about stew. You do work on the front and back ends, but mostly the pot just simmers on the stove, making your house smell amazing. Even more lovable are the easy free-form dumplings in this hearty recipe, in which chicken and dumplings meets coq au vin.

CHICKEN STEW

Crisp bacon in a large Dutch oven over medium heat; transfer to a paper towel–lined plate.

Place flour in a shallow bowl. Season chicken with salt and pepper and dredge in flour. Working in batches, cook chicken, skin side down, in same pot over medium heat until deep golden brown and crisp (do not turn), 12–15 minutes. Transfer to a plate.

Working in 2 batches, cook mushrooms in same pot, seasoning with salt and pepper and stirring occasionally, until brown, 5–8 minutes. Transfer to a bowl. Add onion and garlic to pot; cook, stirring occasionally, until onion is soft and translucent, 5–8 minutes.

Add wine to pot; simmer until reduced by half, about 5 minutes. Add chicken, bacon, thyme, bay leaves, and broth; season with salt and pepper. Bring to a boil, reduce heat, and gently simmer, partially covered, skimming occasionally, until chicken is falling off the bone, 2–2½ hours. Add mushrooms and simmer until flavors meld, 10–15 minutes; season with salt and pepper.

DUMPLINGS AND ASSEMBLY

Bring a pot of salted water to a boil. Whisk flour, baking powder, nutmeg, pepper, and ¾ tsp. salt in a medium bowl. Whisk in eggs and milk. Reduce heat until water is at a strong simmer. Drop teaspoonfuls of batter into water; cook until dumplings are cooked through and doubled in size, 5 minutes. Remove with slotted spoon; add to stew just before serving. **DO AHEAD:** Stew (without dumplings) can be made 3 days ahead.

Let's Go Dutch

A Dutch oven should last forever, so make sure it's the right one. Le Creuset's reputation is unmatched, but which shape and size are best? The *BA* Test Kitchen swears by the 7¼-quart round French oven: It's ideal for family-size stews (the next size up dwarfs them), and the round style lines up with stove-top burners (no cold spots). As for color, we like Flame, but we won't hold you to it. Look on eBay for all sorts of vintage hues.

INDIAN-SPICED CHICKEN with TOMATO and CREAM

6 SERVINGS

- 3 Tbsp. ghee (clarified butter) or vegetable oil
- 6 chicken legs (drumsticks with thighs; about 3 lb.)
- Kosher salt, freshly ground black pepper
- 1 medium onion, finely chopped
- 4 garlic cloves, finely grated
- 2 Tbsp. finely grated peeled ginger
- 2 Tbsp. tomato paste
- 2 tsp. garam masala
- 2 tsp. ground cumin
- 2 tsp. ground turmeric
- 1½ tsp. ground coriander
- ¾ tsp. cayenne pepper
- ¾ tsp. ground cardamom
- 8 cups low-sodium chicken broth
- ¾ cup canned tomato purée
- ½ cup heavy cream
- 1 lb. small Yukon Gold potatoes, sliced ¼" thick
- Plain yogurt, torn fresh mint, and naan, flatbread, or cooked rice (for serving)

This fragrant sauce calls for a mix of dried spices. If the ones you've got in the pantry smell musty or you can't remember when you bought them, it's time to restock.

Heat ghee in a large Dutch oven over medium heat. Season chicken with salt and pepper. Working in batches, cook chicken, skin side down, until golden brown (do not turn), 8–10 minutes. Transfer to a plate.

Add onion, garlic, and ginger to pot and cook, stirring occasionally, until onion is very soft and golden brown, 8–10 minutes. Add tomato paste, garam masala, cumin, turmeric, coriander, cayenne, and cardamom and cook, stirring often, until tomato paste is beginning to darken, about 4 minutes.

Add chicken, broth, tomato purée, and cream to pot; season with salt and pepper. Bring to a boil, reduce heat, and simmer, partially covered, skimming occasionally, until chicken is almost falling off the bone and liquid is slightly thickened, 1½–2 hours.

Add potatoes to pot and cook, partially covered, until potatoes are fork-tender, chicken is falling off the bone, and liquid is thick enough to coat a spoon, 30–45 minutes. Remove skin and bones from chicken, if desired, and return meat to pot; season stew with salt and pepper.

Divide stew among bowls, top with yogurt and mint, and serve with naan, flatbread, or rice.

DO AHEAD: Stew can be made 3 days ahead. Let cool; cover and chill.

What olive oil is to Italian food, ghee is to Indian cuisine. Spoon it onto steamed rice, use it to grease the griddle for pancakes, and sub it for oil in curries and soups.

ROAST DUCKS
WITH POTATOES, FIGS,
AND ROSEMARY
P. 108

ROAST DUCKS
with POTATOES, FIGS, and ROSEMARY

8 SERVINGS

2 5-lb. whole Pekin ducks

2 large onions, quartered

1 large bunch rosemary, divided

Kosher salt, freshly ground
black pepper

3 lb. small Yukon Gold potatoes,
peeled

2 pints fresh black Mission
or Turkish figs, halved

Roasting a whole duck can seem daunting (the size! the fat!), but a burnished roast bird is easily within reach. And the duck fat it yields: liquid gold. This elegant recipe might just replace your centerpiece roast.

Preheat oven to 425°. Set ducks, breast side down, on a work surface and score fatty areas along backs and thighs with a paring knife, being careful not to cut into flesh. Turn over and score fat, concentrating mainly on breasts but extending to tops of legs. Poke a few holes around extra-fatty areas of cavity.

Stuff ducks with onions and all but 4 sprigs rosemary; season generously with salt and pepper (much of the seasoning will melt away as the fat renders).

Place ducks, breast side down, in a large roasting pan; pour in ½ cup water. Roast, rotating pan occasionally, until duck fat starts to render, water is evaporated, and skin is golden brown, about 40 minutes. Remove pan from oven and transfer ducks to a platter or baking dish. Carefully pour rendered fat into a heatproof measuring cup.

Toss potatoes and ¼ cup duck fat in roasting pan (save remaining fat for another use); season with salt and pepper. Scoot potatoes to perimeter and return ducks to pan, breast side up. Roast until potatoes and dark meat are tender and an instant-read thermometer inserted into breasts registers 155°, 50–60 minutes. Transfer ducks to a cutting board; let rest at least 10 minutes before carving.

Meanwhile, add figs and remaining 4 rosemary sprigs to pan; toss well. Roast until figs are soft and juicy, 5–8 minutes. Serve duck with figs and potatoes.

Duck School

A Pekin (a.k.a. Long Island) duck is best for roasting whole: It is the ideal size and has sweet meat and good fat content. Many purveyors stock the birds frozen, so pick them up a day or two before cooking.

SCORE IT
There's a ton of wonderful fat layered between the skin and meat of the duck— more than you'll want to eat. So it's crucial to score the breasts and legs, slicing through the skin and fat, stopping before you hit the meat, to allow some of that goodness to render out.

USE THAT RENDERED FAT
Store in the fridge and use to roast indulgent potatoes and veg, sear lean meats (to add richness), and crisp up the ultimate fried eggs.

NASHVILLE-STYLE HOT CHICKEN

8 SERVINGS

2 3½–4-lb. chickens, each cut into 10 pieces (breasts halved)

1 Tbsp. freshly ground black pepper

2 Tbsp. plus 4 tsp. kosher salt

4 large eggs

2 cups buttermilk or whole milk

2 Tbsp. vinegar-based hot sauce (such as Tabasco or Texas Pete)

4 cups all-purpose flour

Vegetable oil (for frying; about 10 cups)

6 Tbsp. cayenne pepper

2 Tbsp. dark brown sugar

1 tsp. chili powder

1 tsp. garlic powder

1 tsp. paprika

White bread and sliced pickles (for serving)

SPECIAL EQUIPMENT: A deep-fry thermometer

Restaurants around the country are featuring the Nashville specialty hot chicken—and with good reason: It's as delicious as it is spicy (and it's *very* spicy). No doubt about it, six tablespoons of cayenne is a lot, but that's what Hattie B's in Nashville considers "medium." For a milder heat, decrease to two tablespoons. Serve with white bread to help quell the flames.

Toss chicken with black pepper and 2 Tbsp. salt in a large bowl. Cover and chill at least 3 hours.

Whisk eggs, buttermilk, and hot sauce in a large bowl. Whisk flour and remaining 4 tsp. salt in another large bowl.

Fit a Dutch oven with thermometer; pour in oil to measure 2". Heat over medium-high heat until thermometer registers 325°. Pat chicken dry. Working with 1 piece at a time, dredge in flour mixture, shaking off excess, then dip in buttermilk mixture, letting excess drip back into bowl. Dredge again in flour mixture and place on a baking sheet.

Working in 4 batches and returning oil to 325° between batches, fry chicken, turning occasionally, until skin is deep golden brown and crisp and an instant-read thermometer inserted into thickest part of pieces registers 160° for white meat and 165° for dark, 15–18 minutes. Transfer to a clean wire rack set inside a baking sheet. Let oil cool slightly.

Whisk cayenne, brown sugar, chili powder, garlic powder, and paprika in a medium bowl; carefully whisk in 1 cup frying oil. Brush fried chicken with spicy oil. Serve with bread and pickles.

DO AHEAD: Chicken can be seasoned 1 day ahead. Keep chilled.

NASHVILLE-STYLE
HOT CHICKEN
P. 109

PAN-ROASTED CHICKEN with HARISSA CHICKPEAS

4 SERVINGS

1 Tbsp. olive oil

8 skin-on, bone-in chicken thighs (about 3 lb.)

Kosher salt, freshly ground black pepper

1 small onion, finely chopped

2 garlic cloves, finely chopped

2 Tbsp. tomato paste

2 15-oz. cans chickpeas, rinsed

¼ cup harissa paste

½ cup low-sodium chicken broth

¼ cup chopped fresh flat-leaf parsley

Lemon wedges, for serving

INGREDIENT INFO: Harissa, a spicy North African red chile paste, is available at Middle Eastern markets, some specialty foods stores, and online.

The Middle Eastern spice paste harissa is a great shortcut ingredient to flavor, but no two jars (or tubes) are the same. Taste first—if it seems very spicy, use a bit less. You can always stir more into the chickpeas when the dish is finished.

Preheat oven to 425°. Heat oil in a large ovenproof skillet over medium-high heat. Season chicken with salt and pepper. Working in 2 batches, cook until browned, about 5 minutes per side; transfer to a plate.

Pour off all but 1 Tbsp. drippings from pan. Add onion and garlic; cook, stirring often, until softened, about 3 minutes. Add tomato paste and cook, stirring, until beginning to darken, about 1 minute. Add chickpeas, harissa, and broth; bring to a simmer.

Nestle chicken, skin side up, in chickpeas; transfer skillet to oven. Roast until chicken is cooked through, 20–25 minutes. Top with parsley and serve with lemon wedges for squeezing over.

Browning chicken has an often-overlooked payoff: As the meat cooks, the fat under the skin renders, infusing the dish with soul-satisfying flavor. In this recipe, you'll end up with more of those delicious drippings than you'll need. Don't let that goodness go to waste! Drain off the excess and sub it for oil in a warm mustard vinaigrette. The rich dressing is great with greens—especially sturdy ones like escarole, which is excellent alongside this chicken.

GARLIC-and-ROSEMARY GRILLED CHICKEN with SCALLIONS

4 SERVINGS

1 3½–4-lb. chicken, backbone removed

Kosher salt, freshly ground black pepper

4 sprigs rosemary

2 heads of garlic, halved crosswise

2 bunches red scallions

2 Tbsp. olive oil, divided

1 Tbsp. onion or chive blossoms (optional)

Make sure you keep your grill at a steady medium-level heat; if it's too hot, the chicken will char without cooking through, says Carlo Mirarchi, the chef at Roberta's in Brooklyn. Don't worry about the aromatics, though: They're meant to be blackened and then discarded.

Prepare grill for medium heat. Season chicken with salt and pepper. Place rosemary, garlic, and 1 bunch of scallions in a layer on grill.

Place chicken, skin side up, on top of aromatics. Cover grill and cook until chicken is nearly cooked through, 35–40 minutes (aromatics will be thoroughly charred).

Brush chicken with 1 Tbsp. oil and place skin side down, directly onto grates (you can discard aromatics at this point). Grill until chicken is cooked through and skin is crisp, 10–15 minutes longer. Transfer to a cutting board and let rest 10 minutes before cutting into pieces.

Meanwhile, toss remaining bunch of scallions with remaining 1 Tbsp. oil on a rimmed baking sheet and grill until tender and lightly charred, about 5 minutes.

Serve chicken with grilled scallions alongside, topped with onion blossoms, if desired.

MASSAMAN CHICKEN

8 SERVINGS

1 Tbsp. vegetable oil

1 4–4½-lb. chicken, cut into
   10 pieces

   Kosher salt

4 medium Yukon Gold potatoes
   (about 1½ lb.), quartered

2 medium red onions,
   cut into wedges

¾ cup prepared massaman
   curry paste

12 oz. Belgian-style wheat beer

4 13.5-oz. cans unsweetened
   coconut milk

2 cups low-sodium chicken broth

½ cup fish sauce

¼ cup fresh lime juice

1 Tbsp. palm or light brown sugar

1 tsp. red chile powder

   Freshly ground black pepper

   Cilantro sprigs, fried shallots,
   and cooked rice (for serving)

If you're making this nuanced Thai curry from New York's Uncle Boons ahead, reheat it gently about 45 minutes before you plan to serve it, stirring infrequently so that the potatoes stay intact.

Heat oil in a large heavy pot over medium-high heat. Season chicken with salt and cook in batches, skin side down, until golden brown (do not turn), 8–10 minutes; transfer to a plate.

Cook potatoes in same pot, turning occasionally, until brown, 8–10 minutes; transfer to another plate. Cook onions in pot, stirring occasionally, until golden brown, 5–8 minutes; transfer to plate with potatoes.

Add curry paste to pot and cook, stirring, until fragrant, about 4 minutes. Add beer. Bring to a boil, reduce heat, and simmer until reduced by half, 5–7 minutes. Add chicken, coconut milk, and broth. Bring to a boil, reduce heat, and simmer until chicken is very tender, 1–1½ hours.

Return potatoes and onions to pot and cook until potatoes are soft, about 30 minutes. Remove from heat and mix in fish sauce, lime juice, palm sugar, and chile powder; season with salt and pepper. Top with cilantro and shallots. Serve with rice.

DO AHEAD: Chicken can be made 2 days ahead. Cover and chill.

They make Thai curry paste from scratch at Uncle Boons, but we wanted to know what co-chef Ann Redding would use at home. The authentic-tasting Maesri Thai brand is her favorite.

HERBED FAUX-TISSERIE CHICKEN and POTATOES

4 SERVINGS

2 tsp. fennel seeds

1 tsp. crushed red pepper flakes

2 Tbsp. finely chopped fresh marjoram; plus 4 sprigs, divided

2 Tbsp. finely chopped fresh thyme; plus 4 sprigs, divided

1 Tbsp. kosher salt, plus more

½ tsp. freshly ground black pepper, plus more

6 Tbsp. olive oil, divided

1 3½–4-lb. chicken

1 lemon, quartered

1 head of garlic, halved crosswise

2 lb. Yukon Gold potatoes, scrubbed, halved, or quartered if large

You can roast a chicken in less time, but going low-and-slow yields a meltingly tender, shreddable texture. Any spice—aniseed, coriander, crushed chile flake—will work in the rub. And the potatoes, roasting in all that flavor-infused chicken fat? Oh, man.

Preheat oven to 300°. Coarsely grind fennel seeds and red pepper flakes in a spice mill or with a mortar and pestle. Combine spice mixture, chopped marjoram, chopped thyme, 1 Tbsp. salt, ½ tsp. pepper, and 3 Tbsp. oil in a small bowl. Rub chicken inside and out with spice mixture. Stuff chicken with lemon, garlic, 2 marjoram sprigs, and 2 thyme sprigs. Tie legs together with kitchen twine.

Toss potatoes with remaining 3 Tbsp. oil on a rimmed baking sheet; season with salt and pepper. Push potatoes to edges of baking sheet and scatter remaining 2 marjoram and 2 thyme sprigs in center; place chicken on herbs. Roast, turning potatoes and basting chicken every hour, until skin is browned, meat is extremely tender, and potatoes are golden brown and very soft, about 3 hours. Let chicken rest at least 10 minutes before carving.

ZA'ATAR ROAST CHICKEN with GREEN TAHINI SAUCE

6 SERVINGS

GREEN TAHINI SAUCE

2 garlic cloves, smashed

1 cup (lightly packed) flat-leaf parsley leaves with tender stems

½ cup tahini

¼ cup fresh lemon juice

Kosher salt

CHICKEN AND ASSEMBLY

1 3½–4-lb. chicken, cut into quarters, or 2 large skin-on, bone-in chicken breasts and 2 skin-on, bone-in chicken legs

2 medium red onions, thinly sliced

2 garlic cloves, smashed

1 lemon, thinly sliced, seeds removed

1 Tbsp. sumac

1½ tsp. ground allspice

1 tsp. ground cinnamon

1 cup low-sodium chicken broth or water

¼ cup olive oil, plus more for drizzling

Kosher salt, freshly ground black pepper

2 Tbsp. za'atar

2 Tbsp. unsalted butter

¼ cup pine nuts

6 pieces lavash or other flatbread

INGREDIENT INFO: Sumac and za'atar are available at Middle Eastern markets and specialty foods stores, and online.

This dish is from London chef and cookbook author Yotam Ottolenghi. Because of the brothy marinade, he explains, the skin won't get as crisp as with other roast chickens, but the flesh will be so tender, you'll want to eat it with your hands. (Or flatbread.) The Green Tahini Sauce is delicious on just about everything.

GREEN TAHINI SAUCE

Pulse garlic, parsley, tahini, lemon juice, and ½ cup water in a food processor, adding more water if needed, until smooth (sauce should be the consistency of a thin mayonnaise); season with salt.

DO AHEAD: Sauce can be made 1 day ahead. Cover and chill.

CHICKEN AND ASSEMBLY

Preheat oven to 400°. Toss chicken, onions, garlic, lemon, sumac, allspice, cinnamon, broth, and ¼ cup oil in a large resealable plastic bag; season with salt and pepper. Chill at least 2 hours.

Place chicken, onions, garlic, and lemon on a rimmed baking sheet, spooning any remaining marinade over and around chicken. Sprinkle with za'atar and roast until chicken is browned and cooked through, 45–55 minutes.

Meanwhile, melt butter in a small skillet over medium-high heat. Add pine nuts and cook, stirring often, until butter foams, then browns, and nuts are golden brown (be careful not to burn), about 4 minutes; season with salt.

Slice chicken breasts, if desired. Serve chicken with roasted onion and lemon, topped with pine nuts, with green tahini sauce and lavash.

DO AHEAD: Chicken can be marinated 1 day ahead. Keep chilled.

3

seafood

MACKEREL with CRUSHED POTATOES and OREGANO

4 SERVINGS

2 lb. small waxy potatoes
   (such as baby Yukon Gold)

Kosher salt

1 cup plain whole-milk
   Greek yogurt

1 tsp. (or more) fresh lemon juice

1 tsp. white wine vinegar

Freshly ground black pepper

4 garlic cloves, peeled, crushed

5 Tbsp. olive oil, divided

4 6-oz. skin-on mackerel fillets

2 Tbsp. fresh oregano leaves

1 tsp. finely grated lemon zest

Flaky sea salt (such as Maldon)

* **ALSO TRY IT WITH:** Black bass, branzino, snapper, or trout fillets

If you worry that mackerel is too fishy, this is the recipe that will change your mind. The fish's assertive, slightly oily character is tempered by the brightness of lemon juice and creamy richness of yogurt.

Place potatoes in a large pot, add water to cover, and season with kosher salt. Bring to a boil, reduce heat, and simmer until tender, 10–12 minutes. Drain; let cool slightly.

Meanwhile, preheat broiler. Whisk yogurt, lemon juice, and vinegar in a small bowl; season with kosher salt and pepper. Set yogurt sauce aside.

Place potatoes on a broilerproof rimmed baking sheet and, using the bottom of a small bowl or measuring cup, press potatoes to flatten slightly. Add garlic, drizzle with 4 Tbsp. oil, and toss to coat; season with kosher salt and pepper. Broil potatoes until golden brown, 10–12 minutes.

Rub skin side of mackerel with remaining 1 Tbsp. oil; season with kosher salt and pepper. Place, skin side up, on top of potatoes and broil until fish is opaque throughout and skin is crisp, 10–12 minutes. Remove from oven and top with oregano and lemon zest.

Spoon yogurt sauce onto each plate and top with potatoes and fish; sprinkle with sea salt.

Download Monterey Bay Aquarium's Seafood Watch app onto your smartphone and use it while shopping to ensure you're making a sustainable choice. You may have to ask your fishmonger where the fish comes from, but it will help inform your decision. Fish from the U.S., for example, are often a good choice, because the waters are tightly regulated.

SEARED HAKE with BABY POTATOES and GREEN SAUCE

4 SERVINGS

GREEN SAUCE

⅓ cup fresh celery juice (from about 2 stalks)

⅓ cup fresh sorrel or cilantro juice (from about 2 cups, lightly packed)

2 tsp. fresh leek juice (from about 1 dark-green leek top)

1 Tbsp. white wine vinegar or lemon juice

Kosher salt

FISH, POTATOES, AND ASSEMBLY

1 lb. peanut potatoes or baby potatoes (as small as possible)

Kosher salt

3 Tbsp. olive oil, divided, plus more for drizzling

4 4-oz. pieces skin-on hake or cod fillet

4 scallions, trimmed

½ cup plain Greek yogurt

Chervil or other tender herb sprigs (for serving)

The balance of this bright, supremely fresh green sauce, developed by Ignacio Mattos at New York's Estela, is all in the mix. Sorrel is citrusy, but can be quite sharp. Celery is cooling, and the leeks deliver structure and heat. Start your juicer!

GREEN SAUCE

Juice each ingredient separately. Combine celery, sorrel, and leek juices and vinegar in a small bowl; season with salt and more vinegar, if desired. DO AHEAD: Green juice without vinegar can be made 6 hours ahead. Cover and chill. Stir in vinegar just before serving.

FISH, POTATOES, AND ASSEMBLY

Place potatoes in a medium saucepan and add water to cover; season with salt. Bring to a boil, reduce heat, and simmer until tender, 10–15 minutes; drain and return to saucepan. Toss potatoes with 1 Tbsp. oil, then season with salt.

Meanwhile, heat 1 Tbsp. oil in a large skillet over medium-high heat. Season fish with salt and cook, skin side down, until very crisp, about 4 minutes. Turn fish and cook until just cooked through, about 2 minutes longer. Transfer to a plate.

Heat remaining 1 Tbsp. oil in same skillet and add scallions. Cook, turning occasionally, until scallions are charred in spots and are slightly softened, about 1 minute. Transfer to plate with fish.

Divide fish, yogurt, and potatoes among shallow bowls. Spoon green sauce around and drizzle with oil. Top with scallions and chervil.

How to Turn That Juice into a Sauce

A bracing green juice is the perfect post-indulgence drink, but in the hands of a chef, a similar elixir can elevate a dish as handily as any fancy reduction. We love Mattos's master sauce recipe, but to make your own, start with something acidic (Mattos loves sorrel), add an oniony note (chives, leeks), and go from there. Blend juices to taste.

1

JUICE

Run herbs and vegetables through juicer separately. Combine juices to taste, adding vinegar or lemon juice for brightness. (Pickle juice is great and adds flavor, too.)

2

SERVE

Place protein in a shallow bowl; mix up the sauce and then spoon it around protein. Drizzle sauce with olive oil for a luxe look.

STIR-FRIED GRAINS with SHRIMP and EGGS

4 SERVINGS

4 shallots, thinly sliced

2 star anise pods (optional)

½ dried chile de árbol or ½ tsp. crushed red pepper flakes

5 Tbsp. vegetable oil, divided

Kosher salt

12 oz. deveined peeled rock shrimp, or large shrimp, cut into ¾" pieces

4 garlic cloves, finely chopped

2 Tbsp. chopped peeled ginger

2⅓–3 cups cooked grains (such as sorghum, semi-pearled farro, or barley)

1 Tbsp. soy sauce

1 Tbsp. unseasoned rice vinegar

2 tsp. toasted sesame oil

4 large eggs

1 red chile, with seeds, thinly sliced into rounds

1 cup fresh cilantro, basil, and/or mint leaves

Make extra grains on Sunday and use them for this lightning-quick weeknight dinner.

Combine shallots, star anise, if using, chile de árbol, and 3 Tbsp. vegetable oil in a large wok or skillet and cook over medium-high heat, stirring often, until shallots are golden, about 5 minutes. Using a slotted spoon, transfer to a paper towel–lined plate; discard star anise and red chile. Season shallots with salt.

Increase heat to high; cook shrimp, garlic, and ginger in wok, tossing, until shrimp are cooked through, about 3 minutes. Transfer to another plate.

Heat 1 Tbsp. vegetable oil in wok; add grains, pressing evenly against bottom and sides of wok. Cook until grains crackle, about 1 minute; toss and press against pan again. Cook until lightly toasted, about 4 minutes. Add shrimp, soy sauce, vinegar, and sesame oil. Cook, tossing, until liquid is absorbed, about 1 minute.

Heat remaining 1 Tbsp. vegetable oil in a medium nonstick skillet over medium-high heat. Fry eggs until whites are set but yolks are still runny, about 3 minutes. Top grains with eggs, crispy shallots, red chile, and herbs.

SLOW-ROASTED
SALMON WITH
FENNEL, CITRUS,
AND CHILES
P. 132

SALT-BAKED
SALMON WITH
CITRUS
AND HERBS
P. 133

SLOW-ROASTED SALMON with FENNEL, CITRUS, and CHILES

6 SERVINGS

1 medium fennel bulb, thinly sliced

1 blood or navel orange, very thinly sliced, seeds removed

1 Meyer or regular lemon, very thinly sliced, seeds removed

1 red Fresno chile or jalapeño, with seeds, thinly sliced

4 sprigs dill, plus more for serving

Kosher salt, coarsely ground black pepper

1 2-lb. skinless salmon fillet, preferably center-cut

¾ cup olive oil

Flaky sea salt (such as Maldon)

* **ALSO TRY IT WITH:** Cod, halibut, John Dory, or turbot fillets

This low-heat method is very gentle, lending the salmon a velvety texture. Don't bother trying to divide this fillet into tidy portions, says Seattle chef Renee Erickson of The Whale Wins. Instead, use a spoon to break it into perfectly imperfect pieces.

Preheat oven to 275°. Toss fennel, orange slices, lemon slices, chile, and 4 dill sprigs in a shallow 3-qt. baking dish; season with kosher salt and pepper. Season salmon with kosher salt and place on top of fennel mixture. Pour oil over.

Roast until salmon is just cooked through (the tip of a knife will slide through easily and flesh will be slightly opaque), 30–40 minutes for medium-rare.

Transfer salmon to a platter, breaking it into large pieces as you go. Spoon fennel mixture and oil from baking dish over; discard dill sprigs. Season with sea salt and pepper and top with fresh dill sprigs.

How to Buy Wild Salmon

Wild salmon isn't cheap, but it's worth it. It's a fish you can feel good about eating, and not just because it's delicious. Here are a few points to consider next time you're making choices at the fish counter:

In terms of taste, wild salmon is richer, with a deeper flavor than farmed. The absence of color-boosting dyes means the vivid orange flesh you're looking at is the real thing. And that fresh, salty flavor? It comes from the ocean, not an added saline solution.

Like baseball and tomatoes, salmon has a season. Most wild salmon spawn in summer and are at their fit, fat, flavorful best before swimming upstream to reproduce. Look for fresh wild salmon from May through September. Out of season, frozen wild salmon (often sold thawed) is your best bet.

Both wild and farmed salmon are heart-healthy, rich in omega-3 fatty acids. But farmed salmon can be contaminated with PCBs, heavy metals, and pesticide residue, and carries plenty of environmental baggage.

SALT-BAKED SALMON with CITRUS and HERBS

8 SERVINGS

SALMON

- 1 5–6-lb. head- and tail-on salmon or arctic char, cleaned
- 10 cups kosher salt (from about one 48-oz. box), plus more
- 1 grapefruit, thinly sliced
- 2 lemons, thinly sliced
- ½ bunch dill
- ½ bunch tarragon

BEURRE BLANC AND ASSEMBLY

- 1 small shallot, finely chopped
- ½ cup dry white wine
- ¾ cup (1½ sticks) chilled unsalted butter, cut into pieces
- 2 Tbsp. crème fraîche
- 1 tsp. finely grated grapefruit zest
- 1 tsp. fresh grapefruit juice
- 1 tsp. finely grated lemon zest
- 3 tsp. fresh lemon juice, divided
  Kosher salt
- 1 cup fresh parsley leaves with tender stems
- ⅓ cup fresh dill leaves
- ⅓ cup fresh tarragon leaves
- 2 Tbsp. chopped capers
- 2 tsp. caraway seeds

SOURCING INFO: Salmon will be closer to 5 lb.; arctic char closer to 6 lb. Not all shops will have whole fish this large on hand; call ahead so they can order it.

Baking a whole fish in a salt crust ensures super-moist flesh. But if your fish is on the smaller side, just make sure to take it out of the oven on the lower end of the time range.

SALMON

Place a rack in the center of oven and preheat to 400°. Season inside of salmon with salt. Stuff with one-third of grapefruit slices, lemon slices, dill sprigs, and tarragon sprigs.

Mix 10 cups salt and 1½ cups water in a large bowl, adding more water as needed, until mixture is the texture of wet sand. Spread a thin layer of salt mixture on a rimmed baking sheet roughly the same shape and size as fish.

Top salt mixture with another third of grapefruit and lemon slices and dill and tarragon sprigs; set salmon on salt bed and top with remaining citrus and herbs. Pack remaining salt mixture over fish, leaving head and tail peeking out.

Roast salmon until just cooked through (poke a paring knife or metal skewer though the salt and into the flesh; it should feel warm to the touch when removed), 40–50 minutes.

BEURRE BLANC AND ASSEMBLY

While salmon is cooking, simmer shallot and wine in a small saucepan until only 2 Tbsp. liquid remains, 8–10 minutes. Whisking constantly, add butter a piece at a time, incorporating completely before adding the next piece, to make a glossy, emulsified sauce.

Whisk crème fraîche, grapefruit zest, grapefruit juice, lemon zest, and 1 tsp. lemon juice into sauce; season with salt. Reduce heat to low and keep sauce warm while you finish the dish.

Remove salmon from oven and, using a knife or the edge of a fish spatula, crack salt crust and remove (it should come off in large pieces); let salmon sit 5 minutes before serving.

Meanwhile, toss parsley, dill, tarragon, capers, caraway seeds, and remaining 2 tsp. lemon juice in a medium bowl; season herb salad with salt.

Serve salmon with beurre blanc and herb salad.

ROASTED SALMON
with POTATOES and HERBED
CRÈME FRAÎCHE

4 SERVINGS

POTATOES

1½ lb. small waxy potatoes, scrubbed

Kosher salt

2 Tbsp. olive oil

SALMON AND ASSEMBLY

1 1½-lb. piece skin-on salmon

1 Tbsp. olive oil, plus more for drizzling

Kosher salt

½ cup crème fraîche

2 Tbsp. chopped fresh chives, dill, and/or tarragon, plus tarragon and dill sprigs for serving

2 radishes, trimmed, thinly sliced

Crème fraîche delivers tang along with creamy butterfat to this deconstructed salad by Renee Erickson of Seattle's The Whale Wins; Greek yogurt can be substituted if you wish.

POTATOES

Place potatoes in a medium saucepan and add cold water to cover by 1"; season with salt. Bring to a boil, reduce heat, and simmer until tender, 15–20 minutes; drain and pat dry. Let cool slightly, halve potatoes and toss with oil; season with salt.

SALMON AND ASSEMBLY

Preheat oven to 400°. Place salmon, skin side down, on a parchment-lined rimmed baking sheet; rub with 1 Tbsp. oil and season with salt. Roast until medium-rare (mostly opaque but still slightly translucent in the center), 10–15 minutes. Break up salmon into pieces, removing skin if desired.

Whisk crème fraîche and chopped herbs in a small bowl; season with salt.

Spread herbed crème fraîche on plates and top with salmon, potatoes, radishes, and tarragon and dill sprigs; drizzle with oil.

HALIBUT CONFIT
with LEEKS, CORIANDER, and LEMON

12 SERVINGS

1 Tbsp. coriander seeds, plus
   more very coarsely chopped
   for serving

4 leeks, white and pale-green
   parts only, halved lengthwise,
   cut crosswise into 2" pieces

8 sprigs cilantro, cut
   into 2" pieces, plus
   leaves for serving

1 cup olive oil

1 lemon, thinly sliced,
   seeds removed

   Kosher salt

1 3-lb. skinless halibut fillet,
   halved lengthwise

Ask for a thick center-cut piece of halibut, which makes for the nicest presentation of this elegant, meltingly tender fish.

Preheat oven to 375°. Coarsely grind 1 Tbsp. coriander seeds in a spice mill or with a mortar and pestle. (Alternatively, you can coarsely chop with a knife.)

Toss leeks, cilantro sprigs, oil, half of lemon slices, and 2 tsp. ground coriander in a large roasting pan; season with salt. Roast, tossing occasionally, until leeks are tender and starting to brown, 15–20 minutes. Remove roasting pan from oven and carefully pour infused oil into a large heatproof measuring cup.

Reduce oven temperature to 275°. Season halibut with salt and arrange over leeks in roasting pan. Top with remaining lemon slices and ground coriander and pour infused oil over fish. Roast until halibut is just cooked through and starting to flake, 30–35 minutes.

Cut halibut into large pieces and serve with leeks and lemon topped with chopped coriander seeds and cilantro leaves.

DO AHEAD: Halibut can be roasted 1 hour ahead. Let cool and cover.

With fish, freshness is imperative. So, if possible, shop at a fishmonger that buys directly from a fish market (many supermarkets rely on distributors—an extra middleman). Choose fish that's plump and pristine. The scales of a very fresh whole fish practically sparkle; its eyes should be clear and bright. The gills are feathery and rich red, not matted and brick red. Avoid fillets that appear flat, mushy, or dull or that smell fishy—fresh fish shouldn't smell like much.

SCALLOPS with HAZELNUTS and WARM SUN GOLD TOMATOES

4 SERVINGS

¼ cup coarsely chopped
   skin-on hazelnuts

3 Tbsp. olive oil, divided

   Kosher salt, freshly ground
   black pepper

1½ lb. large sea scallops, side
   muscle removed, patted dry

1 pint Sun Gold or grape tomatoes

1 small shallot, finely chopped

1 Tbsp. white wine vinegar

2 Tbsp. fresh tarragon leaves

When it's too nice out to spend all day at the stove, choose quick-cooking scallops, then add a few of summer's best ingredients.

Preheat oven to 350°. Toast hazelnuts on a rimmed baking sheet, tossing occasionally, until golden brown, 8–10 minutes. Toss with 1 Tbsp. oil; season with salt and pepper.

Meanwhile, heat remaining 2 Tbsp. oil in a large cast-iron or nonstick skillet over medium-high heat until almost smoking. Season scallops with salt and pepper; cook until golden brown and just cooked through, about 3 minutes per side. Transfer to a plate.

Pour off most liquid in skillet. Add tomatoes and shallot, season with salt and pepper, and cook, tossing, until some tomatoes have burst, about 4 minutes. Mix in vinegar and serve with scallops topped with tarragon and hazelnuts.

The Scallop Edge

Beautifully browned scallops are easy to achieve if you know where to start. At the fish counter, ask for additive-free "dry" scallops. ("Wet" scallops are soaked in a preservative that also adds water; they expel liquid as they cook and won't sear as well.) High heat and a hands-off approach take care of the rest.

1

BLOT SCALLOPS DRY WITH PAPER TOWEL

Remove surface moisture before seasoning (do this even if they're "dry"). Preheat a cast-iron pan over medium-high heat.

2

MAKE SURE THE OIL IS HOT

There should be an audible sizzle when you add the scallops. Don't disturb them—you risk tearing the flesh.

3

SEAR FIRST, THEN TURN

Check by peeking underneath. If the underside is browned and scallops release easily, turn to sear the second side.

CRISPY
FISH TACOS
P. 142

CRISPY FISH TACOS

8 SERVINGS

FISH

2 lb. skinless red snapper or other mild white fish fillets

1 cup all-purpose flour

1 cup white rice flour

2 tsp. kosher salt

2 cups club soda

Vegetable oil (for frying; about 8 cups)

ASSEMBLY

16–32 small corn tortillas

Cabbage and Jicama Slaw, Fresno Chile Hot Sauce (for serving; see recipes, page 143)

Sliced avocado, cilantro leaves with tender stems, and lime wedges (for serving)

SPECIAL EQUIPMENT: A deep-fry thermometer

A taco dream come true: crispy, light-as-air fried fish (no, not grilled!), balanced by a creamy slaw and fiery, cooling, and crunchy fixings. We just saved you the trip to Baja.

FISH

Remove any pin bones from fish fillets (using tweezers makes this easy). Cut each fillet in half lengthwise. Cut each half on a diagonal into 1" strips. (Work with the natural shape of the fish as you cut; this will help the pieces stay together instead of falling apart when frying.)

Whisk all-purpose flour, rice flour, and salt in a medium bowl. Gradually whisk in club soda until no lumps remain; adjust with more club soda or rice flour as needed to make it the consistency of thin pancake batter—it should be pourable, but thick enough to coat the fish.

Fit a large pot with a deep-fry thermometer and pour in oil to measure 2". Heat over medium-high heat until thermometer registers 350°.

Working in batches of 5–7 pieces at a time, coat fish in batter, letting excess drip off, then carefully place in oil (to avoid splattering, lower fish into oil pointing away from you). Don't overcrowd the pot: The oil temperature will drop dramatically and fish may stick together.

Fry fish, turning occasionally with a fish spatula or slotted spoon and maintaining oil temperature at 350°, until crust is puffed, crisp, and golden brown, about 5 minutes. Transfer to a wire rack set inside a rimmed baking sheet; season immediately with salt.

ASSEMBLY

While fish is frying, use tongs to heat tortillas one at a time directly over a gas burner, moving them often, until lightly charred and puffed in spots, about 1 minute per side. Transfer to a plate; cover with a clean kitchen towel to keep warm. (If you don't have a gas stove, wrap up a stack of tortillas in a sheet of foil and heat in a 350° oven until warmed through.)

Top tortillas (we like two per taco) with fish, slaw, hot sauce, avocado, cilantro, and jalapeños. Serve with lime wedges.

CABBAGE and JICAMA SLAW

8 SERVINGS

1 bunch cilantro

½ cup sour cream

1 tsp. finely grated lime zest

3 Tbsp. fresh lime juice

½ cup mayonnaise

Kosher salt and freshly ground black pepper

¼ large head of green cabbage, very thinly sliced (about 5 cups)

1 small jicama, peeled, julienned (about 1 cup)

4 scallions, sliced

Separate stems and leaves from cilantro (you should have about ½ cup of each); coarsely chop leaves. Purée cilantro stems, sour cream, lime zest, and lime juice in a blender.

Transfer cilantro mixture to a large bowl and whisk in mayonnaise; season with salt and pepper. Toss in cabbage, jicama, scallions, and chopped cilantro leaves.

FRESNO CHILE HOT SAUCE

MAKES 1 CUP

½ lb. stemmed Fresno chiles (8–10)

6 garlic cloves, peeled

Kosher salt

3 Tbsp. red wine vinegar

Cook chiles and garlic in a large saucepan of boiling salted water until chiles turn bright red, about 2 minutes; drain. Blend chiles, garlic, and vinegar in a blender until almost smooth; season with salt. Let cool.

DO AHEAD: Hot sauce can be made 1 week ahead. Cover and chill.

COD with POTATOES and PRESERVED LEMON RELISH

6 SERVINGS

½ medium onion, unpeeled, halved

½ head garlic (halved crosswise)

1 lemongrass stalk, trimmed, tough outer layers removed, finely chopped

4 sprigs thyme

1 Tbsp. black peppercorns

4 cups low-fat milk

1¼ lb. Yukon Gold potatoes (about 4 large), scrubbed

Flaky gray sea salt or kosher salt

¼ cup plus 3 Tbsp. olive oil

1½ lb. skinless cod fillet, cut into 2" pieces

½ preserved lemon, finely chopped

½ cup finely chopped chives (from about 1 large bunch)

2 Tbsp. fresh lemon juice

1 Tbsp. hot smoked Spanish paprika

For this rustic interpretation of *brandade,* Paris chef Inaki Aizpitarte uses desalinated salt cod, which is not easy to find. We got great results—and the right texture—by simply using fresh cod, but when it comes to the addictive relish spooned over the top, we wouldn't dare change a thing.

Bring onion, garlic, lemongrass, thyme, peppercorns, and milk to a boil in a large saucepan. Reduce heat to low and simmer 20 minutes. Strain infused milk into a medium saucepan. Discard solids.

Meanwhile, cook potatoes in a large pot of boiling salted water until tender, 25–30 minutes. Drain, then peel potatoes and coarsely mash in a large bowl with ¼ cup oil; season with salt.

Bring infused milk just to a boil. Add cod, reduce heat, and simmer until flesh begins to flake and is cooked through, about 5 minutes. Remove cod with a slotted spoon and transfer to a plate.

Combine preserved lemon, chives, lemon juice, paprika, and remaining 3 Tbsp. oil in a small bowl; season relish with salt.

Mix ¼ cup infused milk into potatoes. Place cod over potatoes; spoon relish over.

DO AHEAD: Relish can be made 2 days ahead. Cover and chill.

THE RESTAURANT BEHIND THE RECIPE

Le Chateaubriand

While few outside of the foodist fishbowl know "Ee-NYA-kee," Inaki Aizpitarte is the man nearly every big-name male chef in the world under 40 (or 65) wants to look like, cook like, and be like. The 43-year-old French-Basque chef set out as a landscape designer and ended up outpacing Joël Robuchon on the World's 50 Best Restaurants list. His success comes from Le Chateaubriand, the brasserie with a tasting menu as brashly intellectual and, shall we say, challenging as it is delicious. The first seating has been booked nightly since he and his partners, Franck Audoux and Laurent Cabut, opened the place. The second, no-reservation seating draws so many hopefuls to the now crazily trendy 11th arrondissement that they opened Le Dauphin next door, now a destination in itself, and added a sliver of a wine store in between.

With his naturalist-style plating, bare-bones decor, and fair pricing in a country that has rigorous codes about what restaurants should be, it's no wonder *L'Express* declared the latest crop of arrivals on the Paris food scene "Génération Inaki."

4

vegetarian entrées

SPICY BEANS
and WILTED GREENS

6 SERVINGS

¼ cup plus 1 Tbsp. olive oil, plus
    more for drizzling

4 anchovy fillets packed in oil,
    drained (optional)

4 chiles de árbol or 1 tsp. crushed
    red pepper flakes

4 garlic cloves, thinly sliced

1 large onion, thinly sliced

4 celery stalks, finely chopped

1 sprig rosemary

    Kosher salt, freshly ground
    black pepper

1 Parmesan rind (optional), plus
    shaved Parmesan for serving

1 lb. dried white beans or
    chickpeas, soaked overnight,
    drained

1 bunch kale or mustard greens,
    ribs and stems removed,
    leaves coarsely chopped

1 large bunch flat-leaf spinach,
    trimmed, coarsely chopped

4 cups trimmed arugula
    or watercress, divided

2 tsp. fresh lemon juice

Three humble ingredients have big impact here: The Parmesan rind adds richness, the dried beans deliver creaminess, and anchovies bring the umami. Can't find kale or mustard greens? Collards, Swiss chard, or spinach would be great, too. Just adjust the wilting time a tad.

Heat ¼ cup oil in a large Dutch oven over medium heat. Cook anchovies, if using, chiles, and garlic, stirring occasionally, until garlic is soft and anchovies are dissolved, about 4 minutes. Add onion, celery, and rosemary; season with salt and pepper. Increase heat to medium-high and cook, stirring occasionally, until onion is very soft and golden brown, 8–10 minutes.

Add Parmesan rind, if using, beans, and 10 cups water. Bring to a boil, reduce heat, and simmer, stirring occasionally and adding more water as needed, until beans are beginning to fall apart, 3–4 hours.

Lightly crush some beans to give stew a creamy consistency. Mix in kale, spinach, and half of arugula; season with salt and pepper. Cook until greens are wilted, 5–8 minutes.

Toss remaining arugula with lemon juice and 1 Tbsp. oil; season with salt and pepper. Divide stew among bowls; top with arugula, shaved Parmesan, and a drizzle of oil.

DO AHEAD: Stew can be made 3 days ahead. Let cool; cover and chill.

CARROT PANCAKES with SALTED YOGURT

4 SERVINGS

- 4 large eggs, beaten to blend
- 1 lb. carrots (about 8 medium), peeled, coarsely grated
- ⅓ cup chopped fresh cilantro
- ¼ cup chickpea flour
- Kosher salt, freshly ground black pepper
- 3 Tbsp. (or more) olive oil, divided
- 1 cup plain whole yogurt
- 1 cup spicy greens (such as baby mustard greens, watercress, or arugula)
- 1 Tbsp. fresh lemon juice
- Flaky sea salt (such as Maldon)

Jessica Koslow of Sqirl in Los Angeles creates vegetarian fritters with a texture somewhere between a latke and a pancake. They're also gluten-free. (Thanks, chickpea flour!) We'd eat these for breakfast, lunch, *and* dinner.

Mix eggs, carrots, cilantro, and chickpea flour in a large bowl (mixture will be loose); season with kosher salt and pepper.

Heat 2 Tbsp. oil in a large skillet, preferably cast iron, over medium-high heat. Scoop two ½-cupfuls of carrot mixture into skillet, pressing each to ½" thickness. Cook, rotating skillet occasionally for even browning, until pancakes are golden brown, about 3 minutes per side. Transfer to paper towels to drain. Repeat to make 2 more pancakes, adding more oil to skillet if needed.

Meanwhile, season yogurt with kosher salt and pepper. Toss greens with lemon juice and remaining 1 Tbsp. oil; season with kosher salt and pepper.

Serve carrot pancakes with salad and salted yogurt, seasoned with sea salt and more pepper.

This batter can be made a day ahead. Just keep in mind that it will thicken quite a bit as it sits. If the batter seems too stiff, loosen by whisking in a tablespoon or two of water before firing up your skillet. When cooking the pancakes, be sure to add more oil as needed: It's imperative to developing that golden brown crust.

SWISS CHARD and MUSHROOM GALETTE

4 SERVINGS

WHOLE WHEAT DOUGH

1 cup all-purpose flour

1 cup whole wheat flour

1 tsp. kosher salt

¾ cup (1½ sticks) chilled unsalted butter, cut into pieces

1 Tbsp. apple cider vinegar

GALETTE

1 cup ricotta

Kosher salt, freshly ground black pepper

3 Tbsp. olive oil, divided

4 oz. maitake mushrooms, torn, and/or crimini mushrooms, thinly sliced

1 garlic clove, finely chopped

1 large bunch Swiss chard, ribs and stems removed, leaves cut into bite-size pieces

All-purpose flour (for parchment)

1 large egg, beaten to blend

1 cup mixed fresh tender herbs (such as flat-leaf parsley, cilantro, dill, and/or chives)

1 tsp. finely grated lemon zest

1 tsp. fresh lemon juice

Flaky sea salt (such as Maldon)

Selling skeptics on the idea of a vegetarian dinner is easy when it's in tart form. This whole-wheat dough recipe is also great to have in the freezer for weeknight quiche, crackers, and hand pies.

WHOLE WHEAT DOUGH

Pulse all-purpose flour, whole wheat flour, and salt in a food processor to combine. Add butter and pulse until mixture resembles coarse meal with a few pea-size pieces of butter remaining.

Transfer mixture to a large bowl; drizzle with vinegar and ¼ cup ice water. Mix with a fork, adding more ice water by the tablespoonful if needed, just until a shaggy dough comes together; lightly knead until no dry spots remain (do not overwork). Pat into a disk and wrap in plastic. Chill at least 2 hours.

DO AHEAD: Dough can be made 2 days ahead. Keep chilled.

GALETTE

Preheat oven to 400°. Season ricotta with kosher salt and pepper; set aside.

Heat 1 Tbsp. oil in a large skillet over medium-high heat. Add mushrooms; season with kosher salt and pepper and cook, stirring occasionally, until golden brown and crisp, about 5 minutes. Transfer to a small bowl.

Heat 1 Tbsp. oil in same skillet over medium heat. Cook garlic, stirring, until fragrant, about 30 seconds. Add half of chard, season with kosher salt and pepper, and cook, tossing, until slightly wilted. Add remaining chard and cook, tossing occasionally, until completely wilted, about 4 minutes. Remove from heat; season with salt and pepper. Set aside.

Roll out dough on a lightly floured sheet of parchment to a 14" round about ⅛" thick. Transfer on parchment to a baking sheet. Spread three-fourths of ricotta over dough, leaving a 1½" border. Top with reserved chard, then mushrooms. Dollop remaining ricotta over vegetables. Bring edges of dough up and over filling, overlapping as needed, to create a 1½" border; brush with egg. Bake galette, rotating once, until crust is golden brown and cooked through, 35–40 minutes. Let cool slightly on baking sheet.

Toss herbs with lemon juice and remaining 1 Tbsp. oil in a small bowl; season with pepper. Top galette with herbs, zest, and sea salt.

SWEET POTATO CURRY

12 SERVINGS

1 lemongrass stalk, tough outer layer removed, coarsely chopped

1 2" piece ginger, peeled, chopped

4 garlic cloves

2 Tbsp. vegetable oil

Kosher salt

¼ cup red curry paste

2 Tbsp. tomato paste

1 14.5-oz. can crushed tomatoes

2 13.5-oz. cans coconut milk

1½ lb. sweet potatoes, peeled, cut into 1" pieces

¾ lb. small or young carrots, peeled, cut on a diagonal into 2" pieces

6 medium shallots, peeled keeping roots intact, quartered lengthwise

1 red Thai chile, thinly sliced (optional)

1 Tbsp. fresh lime juice

Steamed jasmine rice (for serving)

Thinly sliced scallions, basil leaves, cilantro leaves with tender stems, and lime wedges (for serving)

This one-dish wonder grants you immunity from even the most gluten-averse, meat-abstaining, fat-conscious dinner guests. The spicy vegetarian curry tastes as good as ever reheated, but you should make the rice on the day you plan to serve this.

Pulse lemongrass, ginger, and garlic in a food processor until very finely chopped.

Heat oil in a large heavy pot over medium heat. Add lemongrass mixture and cook, stirring often, until golden brown, about 5 minutes; season with salt. Add curry and tomato pastes and cook, stirring, until darkened, about 3 minutes. Add tomatoes and cook, scraping up any browned bits, until thickened, about 5 minutes. Stir in coconut milk; season with salt. Bring to a boil; reduce heat and simmer, stirring occasionally, until curry is rich and full of flavor, 20–25 minutes.

Add sweet potatoes and carrots, then pour in water to cover. Partially cover pot and cook until carrots are crisp-tender, 10–15 minutes. Add shallots and cook until potatoes are tender and shallots are soft, 15–20 minutes.

Add chile, if desired, and lime juice to curry and spoon over rice. Top with scallions, basil, and cilantro; serve with lime wedges.

DO AHEAD: Curry can be made 2 days ahead. Let cool; cover and chill.

MUSHROOM PAELLA with KALE and EGGS

MUSHROOM STOCK

- 1 oz. dried porcini mushrooms
- 1 Tbsp. olive oil
- 1 large onion, chopped
- 1 carrot, peeled, chopped
- 1 celery stalk, chopped
- 1 lb. crimini mushrooms, coarsely chopped
- 6 sprigs fresh flat-leaf parsley
- 4 sprigs fresh thyme
- ¼ tsp. black peppercorns
- 1 tsp. kosher salt

PAELLA AND ASSEMBLY

- 6 Tbsp. olive oil, divided
- 1½ lb. crimini mushrooms, quartered
  Kosher salt and freshly ground black pepper
- 1 large onion, very finely chopped
- ½ red bell pepper, very finely chopped
- ½ poblano chile, seeds removed, very finely chopped
- 4 cloves garlic crushed, chopped to a paste
- 1½ cups short-grain Spanish rice (such as Bomba)
- 1 cup dry white wine
- 1 tsp. chopped fresh thyme plus more for serving

"Everything good in life starts with onion and garlic," says Bobby Flay, who created this dish for his New York restaurant Gato. "For paella, always remember to crush the garlic into a paste so it fades into the dish." And the best part of any paella is the crisp layer of rice that forms on the bottom of the pan. Make sure to scrape some out for each portion.

MUSHROOM STOCK

Place porcini mushrooms in a medium bowl and cover with 1 cup boiling water; let sit 30 minutes. Line a fine-mesh sieve with 2 layers of paper towel and set over another medium bowl; pour mushroom mixture through (towels will catch any grit from mushrooms). Set aside porcini mushrooms and soaking liquid.

Heat oil in a large saucepan over medium heat. Cook onion, carrot, and celery, stirring occasionally, until softened, 5–7 minutes. Add crimini mushrooms, parsley, thyme, peppercorns, salt, reserved porcini mushrooms and their soaking liquid, and 6 cups cold water. Bring to a boil, reduce heat, and simmer 30 minutes.

Strain stock into a clean saucepan and keep warm over low heat (you should have about 6 cups).

DO AHEAD: Stock can be made 4 days ahead. Cover and chill. Reheat before using.

PAELLA AND ASSEMBLY

Preheat oven to 425°. Heat 2 Tbsp. oil in a 12" paella pan or skillet over medium-high heat. Cook mushrooms, tossing occasionally, until they release their liquid, about 4 minutes. Continue to cook until liquid evaporates and mushrooms are golden brown and tender, 5–7 minutes longer; season with salt and pepper and transfer to a plate.

(Recipe continued on page 158)

1 bunch small kale, ribs
   and stems removed,
   leaves coarsely chopped
   (about 8 cups)

4 large eggs

¼ cup chopped fresh flat-leaf
   parsley

   Calabrian Chile Oil
   (see recipe, page 159)

Add 2 Tbsp. oil to pan and cook onion, bell pepper, and poblano chile, stirring often, until soft, about 3 minutes. Add garlic and cook, stirring, until fragrant, about 30 seconds; season with salt and pepper.

Add rice and cook, stirring constantly, until rice is translucent, about 3 minutes. Add wine and cook, stirring, until completely evaporated, about 2 minutes. Return mushrooms to pan, stir in 1 tsp. thyme, and add mushroom stock just to cover rice; season with salt and pepper. Cook, without stirring, adding broth as needed to keep rice moist while cooking, until rice is al dente and all liquid is absorbed, 15–20 minutes. (Shake pan after adding more stock to distribute evenly.)

Continue to cook paella, occasionally moving pan around burner to make sure all areas get evenly heated, until a crust (socarrat) forms around the sides and bottom of the pan (rice will smell toasted and make a light crackling sound), 6–8 minutes.

Meanwhile, heat remaining 2 Tbsp. oil in a large skillet over medium-high heat. Add kale, season with salt and pepper, and cook, tossing, until slightly wilted. Add ¼ cup water to skillet and cook kale, tossing, until completely wilted, about 5 minutes longer. Spoon over paella.

Make 4 shallow divots in the top of paella and crack an egg into each divot. Transfer pan to oven and cook paella until egg whites are just set, 8–10 minutes.

Top paella with parsley and more thyme and drizzle with Calabrian Chile Oil. Serve in pan.

Did you buy enough greens? "Cooks always forget kale melts down to nothing," says Bobby Flay. Pick up one bunch for every two diners.

CALABRIAN CHILE OIL

MAKES ABOUT ⅓ CUP

2 Tbsp. finely chopped drained oil-packed Calabrian chiles

½ cup olive oil

Kosher salt and freshly ground black pepper

This versatile oil is a great way to bring heat to just about any dish.

Combine chiles and oil in an airtight container; season with salt and pepper. Cover and chill at least 1 hour.

DO AHEAD: Chile oil can be made 1 week ahead. Keep chilled.

POACHED EGGS
over SCAFATA

4 SERVINGS

1 spring onion bulb, sliced

1 fresh red chile, halved

2 garlic cloves, finely chopped

8 oz. asparagus (about ½ bunch), cut on a diagonal into 1" pieces

¼ cup olive oil, plus more for drizzling

2 scallions, thinly sliced

1 cup fresh fava beans (from about 1 lb. pods) or frozen fava beans, thawed

½ cup shelled fresh peas (from about ½ lb. pods) or frozen peas, thawed

½ head escarole, torn into bite-size pieces (about 2 cups)

¼ cup fresh basil leaves, torn if large

¼ cup fresh mint leaves, torn if large

Kosher salt

2 Tbsp. white wine vinegar

4 large eggs

2 oz. Pecorino Romano, finely grated

If ever there was a dish to make vegetables and eggs look (and taste) decadent, this one is it. Jody Williams, chef of Buvette in New York and Paris, cooks the spring produce in olive oil to deliver deep, luxurious flavor. And she always serves it with toast, whether for breakfast, lunch, or dinner.

Heat onion, chile, garlic, asparagus, and ¼ cup oil in a medium saucepan over medium heat until oil begins to bubble. Reduce heat to medium-low, cover, and cook, shaking pan occasionally, until asparagus is crisp-tender, about 2 minutes. Add scallions, fava beans, and peas; cover and cook until fava beans are just tender, about 2 minutes.

Add escarole, basil, and mint and cook, tossing, until escarole is wilted and asparagus is very tender, about 2 minutes; season with salt.

Meanwhile, bring 2" water to a boil in a large saucepan; reduce heat so water is at a gentle simmer and add vinegar. Crack an egg into a small bowl, then gently slide egg into water. Repeat with remaining eggs, waiting until whites of eggs in water are opaque before adding the next egg (about 30 seconds apart). Poach until whites are set but yolks are still runny, about 3 minutes. Using a slotted spoon, transfer eggs to paper towels as they are done.

Serve scafata topped with eggs and Pecorino and drizzled with oil.

DO AHEAD: Eggs can be poached 2 hours ahead; place in a bowl of ice water and chill. Reheat in barely simmering water 1 minute just before serving.

THE RESTAURANT BEHIND THE RECIPE

Buvette

"Why not?" says Jody Williams when asked why she, a New York City chef, would open a French restaurant in Paris. She started her first venture, Buvette, in Greenwich Village, in early 2011. The entire "*gastrothèque*" is just 1,000 square feet, and guests squeeze behind tables pushed *thisclose* together. The chairs are tiny, the silverware is tiny, and the Gallic fare is—you guessed it—tiny. In the morning, warm croissants come two to an order; in the evening, oxtails are braised and shredded off their bones, then piled onto diminutive slices of toast. The Buvette signature, if you can't tell, is making huge flavors bite-size.

"The response to Buvette in New York fanned the flames," Williams says of her decision to replicate that first restaurant, almost to the letter, in the Pigalle neighborhood of Paris's 9th arrondissement. Along with the recipes, she covered the Parisian bar top with the same marble used in Manhattan and shipped over an identical tin ceiling.

Now Williams's first cookbook, *Buvette: The Pleasure of Good Food*, gives readers the chance to create her dishes at home and read the stories that inspired them—offering a personal glimpse not just inside Buvette, but of Williams herself.

MARINATED TOFU with PEANUTS and CHARRED BEAN SPROUTS

4 SERVINGS

2 14-oz. packages firm tofu, drained, sliced ½" thick

1 jalapeño, with seeds, thinly sliced

½ cup reduced-sodium soy sauce

2 Tbsp. light brown sugar

2 tsp. grated peeled ginger

2 tsp. vegetable oil

2 cups bean sprouts, divided

Kosher salt

Steamed white rice (for serving)

6 scallions, thinly sliced on a diagonal

½ cup chopped salted, roasted peanuts

¼ cup fresh mint leaves

Lime wedges (for serving)

"At home I cook quick, healthy, and vegetarian," says Peter Serpico, chef of Serpico in Philadelphia. Cue this soy-and-ginger-marinated tofu (no cooking required!) that tastes a thousand times better than takeout.

Place tofu on a baking sheet lined with several layers of paper towels; place several layers of paper towels on top and press gently to squeeze out liquid. Cut tofu into ¾"-wide pieces and place in a baking dish.

Whisk jalapeño, soy sauce, brown sugar, and ginger in a small bowl, pour over tofu, and toss to coat. Let sit at least 30 minutes.

Just before serving, heat oil in a medium skillet over medium-high heat. Add 1 cup bean sprouts and cook, undisturbed, until charred, about 3 minutes; season with salt.

Spoon tofu over rice and top with charred and raw bean sprouts, scallions, peanuts, and mint. Serve with lime wedges.

DO AHEAD: Tofu can be marinated 1 hour ahead.

5

pasta, pizza & rice

WINTER SQUASH CARBONARA with PANCETTA and SAGE

4 SERVINGS

- 2 Tbsp. olive oil
- 4 oz. pancetta (Italian bacon), chopped
- 1 Tbsp. finely chopped fresh sage
- 1 2-lb. kabocha or butternut squash, peeled, seeded, cut into ½" pieces (about 3 cups)
- 1 small onion, chopped
- 2 garlic cloves, chopped
  Kosher salt, freshly ground black pepper
- 2 cups low-sodium chicken broth
- 12 oz. fettuccine or linguine
- ¼ cup finely grated Pecorino, plus shaved for serving

This dish is named for its rich and creamy sauce—except it doesn't use a drop of cream or a single yolk. The secret is the squash purée, which gets its silky texture from the squash itself (and, yes, some olive oil).

Heat oil in a large skillet over medium-high heat. Add pancetta, reduce heat to medium, and cook, stirring occasionally, until crisp, 8–10 minutes. Add sage and toss to coat. Using a slotted spoon, transfer pancetta and sage to a small bowl; set aside.

Add squash, onion, and garlic to skillet; season with salt and pepper and cook, stirring occasionally, until onion is translucent, 8–10 minutes. Add broth. Bring to a boil, reduce heat, and simmer until squash is soft and liquid is reduced by half, 15–20 minutes. Let cool slightly, then purée in a blender until smooth; season with salt and pepper. Reserve skillet.

Cook pasta in a large pot of boiling salted water, stirring occasionally, until al dente. Drain, reserving 1 cup pasta cooking liquid.

Combine pasta, squash purée, and ¼ cup pasta cooking liquid in reserved skillet and cook over medium heat, tossing and adding more pasta cooking liquid as needed, until sauce coats pasta, about 2 minutes. Mix in ¼ cup Pecorino; season with salt and pepper.

Serve pasta topped with reserved pancetta and sage, shaved Pecorino, and more pepper.

DO AHEAD: Squash purée can be made 3 days ahead. Let cool; cover and chill.

Butternut and Beyond

With all the varieties of winter squash at the market, choosing the right type for the right dish can be confounding. We're here to help: Each of our three favorites has a particular talent, so play them to their strengths.

BUTTERNUT
Browns beautifully when roasted, enhancing its nutty flavor. Plus, it's resilient (read: It won't turn to mush when cooked).

KABOCHA
Despite its thick, tough skin, kabocha's fine-grained and sweet flesh yields the creamiest (almost potato-like) purée.

DELICATA
Has quick-cooking flesh and thin, edible skin, making it ideal for simply slicing and tossing into soups and stews.

SUNDAY SAUCE with SAUSAGE and BRACIOLE

8 SERVINGS

- 2 cups fresh breadcrumbs
- ½ cup finely grated Pecorino
- ⅓ cup finely chopped fresh flat-leaf parsley
- 1½ tsp. crushed red pepper flakes
- ¼ tsp. hot smoked Spanish paprika
- 7 garlic cloves, finely chopped, divided
- 4 Tbsp. olive oil, divided
- 2 lb. beef top round, thinly sliced by a butcher for braciole
- Kosher salt, freshly ground black pepper
- 2 lb. hot or sweet Italian sausage, halved crosswise
- 1 lb. baby back pork ribs, cut into 3- to 4-rib pieces, or pork spare ribs, cut into individual ribs
- 1 large onion, finely chopped
- 2 anchovy fillets packed in oil, drained
- ¼ cup tomato paste
- 2 28-oz. cans crushed tomatoes
- 2 28-oz. cans whole peeled tomatoes
- 1½ lb. large tubular pasta (such as rigatoni or tortiglioni)

Ask anybody's *nonna*: Making Sunday sauce is not an exact science. You can use other meats—like thick pork chops or short ribs—in place of or in addition to the ones listed here. It's also even better the next day, so go ahead and make this a Saturday sauce.

Spread out breadcrumbs on a baking sheet and let sit uncovered at room temperature until dried out, about 12 hours.

Combine breadcrumbs, Pecorino, parsley, red pepper flakes, paprika, 1 chopped garlic clove, and 2 Tbsp. oil in a medium bowl.

Trim beef slices into 6x2" pieces; season with salt and pepper. Sprinkle each slice with about 2 Tbsp. breadcrumb mixture, roll up, and secure with a toothpick or twine; set braciole aside.

Heat remaining 2 Tbsp. oil in a large heavy pot over medium-high heat and cook sausage until browned on all sides, 5–8 minutes. Transfer to a large rimmed baking sheet. Season ribs with salt and pepper; cook in same pot until browned on all sides, 8–10 minutes. Transfer to baking sheet with sausage. Cook reserved braciole in pot, turning occasionally, until browned, 5–8 minutes; transfer to same baking sheet.

Reduce heat to medium-low and cook onion, anchovy, and remaining garlic in pot, stirring occasionally, until onion is translucent, 8–10 minutes. Add tomato paste and cook, stirring often, until slightly darkened in color, 5–8 minutes. Add crushed and whole tomatoes, crushing whole tomatoes with your hands; season with salt and pepper. Bring to a boil, reduce heat, and simmer, stirring occasionally, until sauce has thickened, 1–1½ hours.

Add sausage, ribs, braciole, and any accumulated juices on baking sheet to sauce. Cook, partially covered, stirring occasionally and skimming surface as needed, until meat is very tender (rib meat should be falling off the bone), 2½–3 hours longer. Season sauce with salt and pepper.

Just before serving, cook pasta in a large pot of boiling salted water, stirring occasionally, until al dente; drain.

Toss pasta in a large bowl with a little of the sauce and top with reserved breadcrumb mixture. Remove bones from ribs and remove toothpicks from braciole. Serve braciole, ribs, sausage, and remaining sauce with pasta alongside.

DO AHEAD: Breadcrumbs can be dried out 5 days ahead; store airtight at room temperature. Sauce can be cooked 2 days ahead; cover and chill. Gently reheat sauce, covered, before cooking pasta.

RICOTTA GNOCCHI
with ASPARAGUS, PEAS,
and MORELS

4 SERVINGS

GNOCCHI

4 cups ricotta (from two
    16-oz. containers)

2 large eggs

1 cup finely grated Parmesan

2 tsp. kosher salt

    Freshly ground black pepper

1 cup all-purpose flour

VEGETABLES AND ASSEMBLY

1 bunch asparagus, trimmed

    Kosher salt

2 Tbsp. olive oil, plus more

¼ lb. fresh morel mushrooms

1 small shallot, finely chopped

1 cup shelled fresh peas
    (from about 1 lb. pods) or
    frozen peas, thawed

¼ cup (½ stick) unsalted butter

    Freshly ground black pepper

    Chopped fresh chives, finely
    grated Parmesan, and
    finely grated lemon zest
    (for serving)

*These ricotta gnocchi are
literally cut to order. Hold the bag
of dough over simmering water
and gently squeeze out about an inch.
Slice flush against the bag
opening and let the dumpling
fall gently into the pot.*

Chef Nemo Bolin at Cook & Brown Public House in Providence, Rhode Island, turned us on to the technique for this streamlined, no-knead gnocchi dough.

GNOCCHI

Line a baking dish with 3 layers of paper towels; spoon ricotta onto paper towels and let sit 20 minutes (if the ricotta is too wet, the dough won't hold together).

Combine ricotta, eggs, Parmesan, and salt in a food processor; season with pepper and process until smooth. Add flour and pulse just to combine (mixture should be smooth and fairly wet). Transfer gnocchi mixture to a pastry bag fitted with ½" round tip or a large resealable plastic bag.

DO AHEAD: Gnocchi mixture can be made 1 day ahead. Cover pastry tip and chill.

VEGETABLES AND ASSEMBLY

Cook asparagus in a large pot of boiling salted water until bright green and crisp-tender, about 1 minute. Using tongs or a mesh strainer, transfer to a bowl of ice water to cool; drain. Slice asparagus on the diagonal into bite-size pieces, leaving tips intact.

Reduce heat so water is simmering. If using a resealable plastic bag for gnocchi mixture, cut a ½" opening in bottom corner of bag. Working in 3 batches, pipe dough into pot, cutting off 1" lengths with a paring knife and letting dough drop into water. Cook until doubled in size, about 3 minutes. Using a slotted spoon, transfer gnocchi to a lightly oiled baking sheet. Reserve ¼ cup cooking liquid.

Heat 2 Tbsp. oil in a large skillet over medium heat. Cook morels, tossing occasionally, until slightly softened, about 5 minutes. Add shallot and cook, tossing occasionally, until shallot and morels are soft, about 5 minutes; set aside.

Add gnocchi, asparagus, peas, butter, and reserved cooking liquid to skillet with morels. Cook, tossing gently, until vegetables are warm and sauce has thickened slightly, about 2 minutes; season with salt and pepper. Serve topped with chives, Parmesan, and lemon zest.

PASTA SHELLS with PROSCIUTTO and LEMON BREADCRUMBS

4 SERVINGS

PROSCIUTTO CREAM

4 oz. prosciutto, cut into ¼" pieces

1 Tbsp. olive oil

1 small shallot, thinly sliced

4 garlic cloves, smashed

¼ cup brandy

2 sprigs thyme

1 bay leaf

Zest of 1 lemon, removed in strips with a vegetable peeler

2 cups heavy cream

BREADCRUMBS

¼ cup olive oil

1 garlic clove

½ cup coarse fresh breadcrumbs

1 tsp. finely grated lemon zest

Kosher salt

ASSEMBLY

4 oz. prosciutto, cut into ¼" pieces

1 Tbsp. olive oil, plus more for serving

12 oz. lumaconi (snail shells) or other medium shell pasta

Kosher salt

1 cup thinly sliced Treviso radicchio

¼ cup coarsely chopped fresh flat-leaf parsley

1 Tbsp. fresh lemon juice

We're obsessed with the snail-shaped pasta *lumaconi* (which is made from scratch at San Francisco's Tosca). You can find it dried from Pastificio G. Di Martino at Whole Foods.

PROSCIUTTO CREAM

Pulse prosciutto in a food processor until finely ground. Heat oil in a large skillet over medium heat. Cook prosciutto, stirring often, until brown and crisp, 5–8 minutes.

Add shallot and garlic to skillet and cook, stirring often, until shallot is soft and garlic is golden brown, about 3 minutes. Add brandy and cook until skillet is almost dry, about 30 seconds.

Add thyme, bay leaf, lemon zest, and cream to skillet and bring to a boil. Reduce heat and simmer until cream is slightly reduced, about 5 minutes. Remove from heat and let steep 30 minutes. Strain through a fine-mesh sieve into a medium bowl; discard solids.
DO AHEAD: Prosciutto cream can be made 1 day ahead. Cover and chill.

BREADCRUMBS

Heat oil in a medium skillet over medium-high heat. Add garlic and cook just until golden, about 2 minutes. Add breadcrumbs and cook, stirring constantly, until golden brown, about 4 minutes. Using a slotted spoon, transfer to paper towels to drain; let cool.

Discard garlic and transfer breadcrumbs to a medium bowl. Add lemon zest and toss to combine; season with salt. **DO AHEAD:** Breadcrumbs (without lemon zest) can be cooked 1 day ahead. Store airtight at room temperature. Add lemon zest just before serving.

ASSEMBLY

Pulse prosciutto in a food processor until finely ground. Heat 1 Tbsp. oil in a large skillet over medium heat. Cook prosciutto, stirring often, until brown and crisp, 5–8 minutes. Add prosciutto cream to skillet and bring to a boil. Reduce heat and simmer, stirring often, until cream is thickened and coats the back of a spoon, about 5 minutes.

Meanwhile, cook pasta in a large pot of boiling salted water, stirring occasionally, until al dente, 8–10 minutes; drain. Add pasta to sauce. Cook over medium heat, tossing, until pasta is well coated, about 2 minutes. Add radicchio, parsley, and lemon juice and toss to combine; season with salt.

Serve pasta topped with breadcrumbs and drizzled with more oil.

LINGUINE and CLAMS with ALMONDS and HERBS

4 SERVINGS

½ cup unsalted, roasted almonds, coarsely chopped

2 Tbsp. finely chopped fresh chives

2 Tbsp. finely chopped fresh flat-leaf parsley

1 Tbsp. plus ¼ cup olive oil

Kosher salt, freshly ground black pepper

4 large garlic cloves, thinly sliced

¾ tsp. crushed red pepper flakes

¼ cup dry white wine

2 lb. littleneck clams, scrubbed

12 oz. linguine

Almonds are the new breadcrumbs. Their toasty flavor and crunch add just the right contrast to almost any plate of pasta—not to mention salads, vegetable sides, and grain bowls.

Mix almonds, chives, parsley, and 1 Tbsp. oil in a small bowl; season with salt and pepper. Set aside.

Heat remaining ¼ cup oil in a large pot over medium heat. Cook garlic and red pepper flakes, stirring occasionally, until garlic is softened, about 2 minutes. Add wine, bring to a boil, and cook until reduced by half, about 2 minutes.

Add clams and increase heat to medium-high; cover pot. Cook, shaking pot occasionally, until clams have opened, 5–8 minutes (discard any that do not open).

Meanwhile, cook pasta in a large pot of boiling salted water, stirring occasionally, until al dente. Drain, reserving 1 cup pasta cooking liquid.

Add pasta and ½ cup pasta cooking liquid to clams and toss to coat. Cook, tossing and adding more cooking liquid as needed, until sauce coats pasta, about 2 minutes; season with salt and pepper.

Serve linguine and clams topped with reserved almond-herb mixture.

SPICY LOBSTER PASTA

4 SERVINGS

12 oz. spaghetti

Kosher salt

2 Tbsp. olive oil

2 Tbsp. unsalted butter

1 large shallot, finely chopped

1 tsp. crushed red pepper flakes

1 lb. cherry and/or Sun Gold tomatoes, halved

1 lb. picked cooked lobster meat or cooked large shrimp

Freshly ground black pepper

1 tsp. finely grated lemon zest

Lemon wedges (for serving)

There's something special about lobster you've prepared yourself, but if cooking one on a weeknight isn't your speed, buy cooked lobster or shrimp instead.

Cook spaghetti in a large pot of boiling salted water, stirring occasionally, until al dente. Drain, reserving 1 cup pasta cooking liquid (the secret to silky sauce).

Meanwhile, heat oil and butter in a large skillet over medium-high heat. Cook shallot and red pepper flakes, stirring often, until shallot is softened, about 2 minutes. Add tomatoes and cook, stirring often, until tomatoes are soft and juicy, 5–8 minutes.

Add lobster meat to skillet and toss to coat. Add pasta and ½ cup reserved pasta cooking liquid; season with salt and pepper. Cook, tossing constantly and adding more reserved pasta cooking liquid as needed, until sauce thickens and coats pasta, about 2 minutes.

Serve pasta topped with lemon zest, with lemon wedges alongside for squeezing over.

FETTUCCINE with SHIITAKES and ASPARAGUS

4 SERVINGS

3 Tbsp. olive oil, divided

1 bunch asparagus, trimmed, cut into 2" pieces

Kosher salt, freshly ground black pepper

2 Tbsp. unsalted butter

8 oz. shiitake mushrooms, stems removed, caps sliced

1 small shallot, finely chopped

1 tsp. chopped fresh oregano

1 tsp. chopped fresh thyme

12 oz. dried or 1 lb. fresh fettuccine

3 oz. Parmesan, grated (about ¾ cup), plus more for serving

4 large egg yolks*

For this seasonal twist on carbonara from Chris Fischer of Beach Plum Restaurant on Martha's Vineyard, stir the yolk into your portion while the pasta is still steaming hot.

Heat 2 Tbsp. oil in a large skillet over medium-high heat. Add asparagus, season with salt and pepper, and cook, stirring occasionally, until just tender, about 4 minutes. Transfer to a plate.

Heat butter and remaining 1 Tbsp. oil in same skillet over medium-high heat. Add mushrooms, season with salt and pepper, and cook, tossing often, until tender, about 5 minutes. Add shallot and cook, tossing occasionally, until softened, about 2 minutes. Toss in oregano, thyme, and asparagus.

Meanwhile, cook pasta in a large pot of boiling salted water, stirring occasionally, until al dente. Drain, reserving 1 cup pasta cooking liquid.

Add pasta, ½ cup pasta cooking liquid, and 3 oz. Parmesan to skillet. Cook, tossing and adding more pasta cooking liquid as needed, until sauce coats pasta, about 2 minutes; season with salt and pepper.

Divide pasta among plates and top each with a yolk and more Parmesan.

*RAW EGG IS NOT RECOMMENDED FOR INFANTS, THE ELDERLY, PREGNANT WOMEN, PEOPLE WITH WEAKENED IMMUNE SYSTEMS...OR PEOPLE WHO DON'T LIKE RAW EGGS.

GRANDMA PIE
P. 182

CLASSIC MOZZARELLA GRANDMA PIE

MAKES 1 PIE (ABOUT 6 SERVINGS)

Grandma-Style Pizza Dough
(see recipe, page 183)

12 oz. fresh mozzarella, grated
(about 2½ cups)

1½ cups Fresh Tomato Pizza Sauce
(see recipe, page 183)

Flaky sea salt (such as Maldon)
and crushed red pepper flakes
(for serving; optional)

A chewy-crisp crust, endless topping ideas, and do-ahead ease. Pizza made in a sheet pan—a.k.a. Grandma Pie—is the simplest, tastiest way to feed a crowd.

Place a rack in lower third of oven and preheat to 525° or as high as oven will go.

Once dough has risen on baking sheet, top with mozzarella and dot pie with tomato sauce; sprinkle with salt and red pepper flakes, if desired. Bake pie until golden brown and crisp on bottom and sides, 20–30 minutes.

That Topping Game

When it comes to toppings, restraint is key. "It's all about ratio," says Frank Pinello of Brooklyn's aptly named Best Pizza, who helped us create this recipe. "You want them to work with the crust, the sauce, the cheese—in balance." We'll even lose the sauce sometimes to make white pies. Here are four of our favorite ways to go Grandma. Get the full recipes at bonappetit.com/pizza.

A	**B**	**C**	**D**
RED ONION	MOZZARELLA	ROASTED CAULIFLOWER	FENNEL
+	+	+	+
BLACK OLIVES	MARINATED TUSCAN KALE	RICOTTA	MOZZARELLA
+	+	+	+
PROVOLONE	RICOTTA	BREADCRUMBS	SPICY SOPPRESSATA

GRANDMA-STYLE PIZZA DOUGH

MAKES ENOUGH DOUGH FOR 1 PIE

1 envelope active dry yeast
   (about 2¼ tsp.)

2 Tbsp. plus ½ cup olive oil,
   plus more for bowl

2 tsp. kosher salt

4 cups all-purpose flour,
   divided, plus more for surface

The second rise is key to the finished pie's texture; if baked too soon, the dough will be firm and too chewy. Make sure it feels floppy, with plenty of puffy air bubbles.

Combine yeast and 1½ cups warm water (105–110°) in a large bowl; let stand until yeast starts to foam, about 10 minutes.

Mix in 2 Tbsp. oil, then salt and 2 cups flour. Add another 2 cups flour, a cup at a time, mixing until incorporated and a shaggy dough forms.

Turn out dough onto a lightly floured surface and knead until soft, smooth, and elastic, 10–12 minutes. Place dough in a lightly oiled bowl and cover with plastic wrap. Chill 24 hours.

Coat an 18x13" rimmed baking sheet with remaining ½ cup oil. Gently and gradually stretch dough until it reaches the edges of baking sheet. (If dough springs back or is stiff to work with, let it rest 10 minutes before continuing. You may need to let it rest more than once.)

Cover dough on baking sheet tightly with plastic wrap and let sit in a warm place (but not too warm—about 70° is ideal for yeast to grow) until it is puffed and full of air bubbles, 30–40 minutes.

FRESH TOMATO PIZZA SAUCE

MAKES ABOUT 5 CUPS

1 28-oz. can whole peeled
   tomatoes, drained

2 anchovy fillets packed in oil,
   drained

2 cloves garlic cloves

6 Tbsp. olive oil

¼ cup fresh basil leaves

   Kosher salt and freshly ground
   black pepper

Save the drained tomato liquid and add to your next vegetable soup or braise, or use in place of water to make tomato rice. You can also freeze it.

Pulse tomatoes, anchovies, garlic, oil, and basil in a food processor or blender until mostly smooth (some texture is okay); season with salt and pepper.

MIGAS FRIED RICE

4 SERVINGS

TEX-MEX JAEW

1 small onion, halved

1 tomatillo, husk removed, rinsed

1 jalapeño

1 dried guajillo or
   New Mexico chile

2 garlic cloves, peeled

1 lemongrass stalk, trimmed,
   tough outer layer removed,
   thinly sliced

2 Tbsp. fish sauce

2 Tbsp. fresh lime juice

2 Tbsp. soy sauce

1 Tbsp. light brown sugar

¾ tsp. ground cumin

RICE AND ASSEMBLY

¼ cup vegetable oil

2 corn tortillas, torn into 1" pieces

1 small onion, finely chopped

1 jalapeño, with seeds,
   finely chopped

   Kosher salt, freshly ground
   black pepper

3 large eggs, beaten to blend

3 cups cooled cooked jasmine rice
   (from 1 cup dry)

2 oz. cheddar, cut into ¼" pieces

2 scallions, thinly sliced

¼ cup fresh cilantro leaves with
   tender stems

   Hot sauce (such as Valentina;
   for serving)

   MSG (optional; for serving)

In this riff on the classic egg-and-tortilla dish, chef Quealy Watson of San Antonio's Hot Joy takes it to a Tex-Mex place in an eggy, cheesy rice dish that might remind you of nachos (trust us, it works).

TEX-MEX JAEW

Roast onion, tomatillo, and jalapeño over a gas burner, turning often, until charred and blistered in spots, about 5 minutes. (Alternatively, broil on a broiler-proof rimmed baking sheet, turning often, 8–10 minutes.)

Meanwhile, toast guajillo chile in a small dry skillet until puffed and fragrant, about 30 seconds per side. Chop chile (with seeds) and transfer to a food processor. Add garlic and lemongrass and pulse to a coarse paste.

Add fish sauce, lime juice, soy sauce, brown sugar, cumin, onion, tomatillo, and jalapeño. Pulse to a coarse purée; season with more fish sauce and lime juice, if desired (mixture should be salty and flavorful).

DO AHEAD: Jaew can be made 1 day ahead. Let cool; cover and chill.

RICE AND ASSEMBLY

Heat oil in a large wok or skillet over medium-high heat. Add tortillas and cook, stirring occasionally, until golden brown and crisp, about 2 minutes. Using a slotted spoon, transfer chips to paper towels to drain. (Alternatively, use store-bought corn chips.)

Increase heat to high and add onion and jalapeño to same wok; season with salt and pepper. Cook, stirring often, until softened and fragrant, about 2 minutes. Add eggs and cook, stirring constantly, until fluffy and just set, about 1 minute. Add rice and cook, stirring often, until rice is evenly coated and beginning to brown, about 4 minutes.

Add jaew and cook, stirring occasionally, until fragrant and paste reduces slightly, about 2 minutes. Remove from heat and mix in cheddar and half of fried tortillas.

Serve fried rice topped with scallions, cilantro, hot sauce, MSG (if using), and remaining fried tortillas.

6

vegetables & sides

SPICE-CRUSTED CARROTS with HARISSA YOGURT

4 SERVINGS

- 2 lb. small carrots, scrubbed, tops trimmed to ½"

  Kosher salt
- 1 Tbsp. sugar
- 1 tsp. English mustard powder
- 1 tsp. hot smoked Spanish paprika
- 1 tsp. ground cumin
- ½ tsp. ground coriander or fennel
- 4 Tbsp. vegetable oil, divided

  Freshly ground black pepper
- ½ cup plain Greek yogurt
- 1 Tbsp. harissa paste
- 2 tsp. chopped fresh thyme, plus more
- ½ tsp. finely grated lemon zest, plus more

  Lemon wedges (for serving)

The sugar in the spice rub of this addictive Bobby Flay dish can burn if cooked too long, so watch these closely as they brown.

Cook carrots in a large pot of boiling salted water until crisp-tender and skins easily rub off, about 5 minutes; drain. Transfer to a bowl of ice water. Using paper towels, gently rub carrots to remove skins and pat dry.

Mix sugar, mustard powder, paprika, cumin, and coriander in a small bowl. Toss carrots with 1 Tbsp. oil in a medium bowl. Add spice mixture; season with salt and pepper and toss to coat.

Heat remaining 3 Tbsp. oil in a large skillet, preferably cast iron. Working in 2 batches, cook carrots, turning occasionally, until deep brown all over, 6–8 minutes; season with salt and pepper.

Meanwhile, place yogurt in a small bowl; season with salt and pepper. Add harissa paste, 2 tsp. thyme, and ½ tsp. lemon zest and gently swirl ingredients, stopping before yogurt turns pink.

Spoon harissa yogurt onto plates and top with carrots, more thyme, and more lemon zest. Serve with lemon wedges.

DO AHEAD: Carrots can be cooked in boiling water and peeled 6 hours ahead. Cover and chill.

Bobby Flay says you're underthinking (and underseasoning) your veg! Flay treats vegetables like he does meat—by seasoning them with abandon. His favorite method is a spice rub, for three reasons: 1. "Rubbing spices into anything gives it a far greater flavor impact." 2. "Rubs form a crust, which helps build texture." 3. "Unlike a marinade, you can cook immediately."

CHARRED SUGAR SNAP PEAS with BUTTERMILK AIOLI

4 SERVINGS

1 small shallot, finely chopped

2 Tbsp. fresh lemon juice

1 large egg yolk

1 garlic clove, finely grated

¼ tsp. kosher salt, plus more
   Pinch of cayenne pepper

½ cup vegetable oil

2 Tbsp. buttermilk

2 Tbsp. crème fraîche
   Freshly ground black pepper

1½ lb. sugar snap peas,
   untrimmed, divided

2 Tbsp. olive oil, divided

1 Tbsp. thinly sliced drained
   oil-packed Calabrian chiles
   Flaky sea salt (such as Maldon)

If you've never charred snap peas on the grill, prepare to become addicted. It couldn't be easier, and they're absolutely delicious. This recipe comes from Carlo Mirarchi, the chef at Brooklyn favorite Roberta's.

Mix shallot and lemon juice in a small bowl. Whisk egg yolk, garlic, kosher salt, cayenne, and 2 tsp. water in a medium bowl. Whisking constantly, gradually drizzle in vegetable oil, drop by drop at first, until aioli is thickened and smooth. Gently mix in buttermilk, crème fraîche, and shallot mixture; season with kosher salt and black pepper.

Prepare grill for medium-high heat. Toss half of snap peas with 1 Tbsp. olive oil in a medium bowl; season with kosher salt and black pepper. Set a wire rack or grill basket on grill grate and grill peas on rack, turning occasionally, until lightly charred, about 4 minutes; return to bowl.

Cut raw peas in half crosswise on a diagonal and toss with grilled peas along with remaining 1 Tbsp. olive oil; season with black pepper. Spoon some aioli on a platter and top with snap peas, chiles, and sea salt. (Reserve remaining buttermilk aioli for another salad, or use it as a dip.)

DO AHEAD: Buttermilk aioli can be made 3 days ahead. Cover and chill.

The aioli will appear quite tight when all the oil is incorporated, but it will loosen to a pourable consistency once the buttermilk and shallot are added.

BRUSSELS SPROUT LEAVES
with CHORIZO
and TOASTED ALMONDS

8 SERVINGS

½ cup skin-on almonds
  (not roasted)

6 oz. Spanish chorizo, thinly sliced

3 Tbsp. olive oil

2 garlic cloves, thinly sliced

2 tsp. fresh thyme leaves

2 lb. brussels sprouts,
  stems trimmed, halved,
  leaves separated

  Kosher salt, freshly ground
  black pepper

1 Tbsp. Sherry vinegar or
  red wine vinegar

A spicy Spanish twist on brussels and bacon done in the style of a stir-fry. Wait till the last minute to pull this dish together—say, while your roast or steak is resting—but have everything prepped and ready to go ahead of time.

Toast almonds in a dry small skillet over medium heat, tossing occasionally, until fragrant and slightly darkened, 5–8 minutes. Let cool, then coarsely chop.

Cook chorizo in a large skillet over medium-high heat, stirring occasionally, until fat starts to render and chorizo is crisp, about 5 minutes. Transfer chorizo to a small bowl and wipe skillet clean (don't skip this step or the reddish-brown chorizo drippings will make brussels sprouts look muddy).

Heat oil in same skillet over medium-high and cook garlic and thyme, stirring occasionally, until garlic is fragrant and golden, about 1 minute. Working in batches, add brussels sprout leaves, tossing and letting them wilt slightly before adding more; season with salt and pepper. Cook, tossing occasionally, until leaves are browned in spots and tender, 8–10 minutes.

Remove from heat and add vinegar, almonds, and chorizo; toss to combine. Season with salt, pepper, and more vinegar, if desired.

Once you've trimmed and halved the brussels sprouts, anyone—a football-watching spouse, a child with passable motor skills—can separate the leaves. Delegate!

GRILLED CHERRY TOMATOES

4 SERVINGS

2 pints ripe cherry tomatoes
   (such as Sun Gold,
   Black Cherry, or teardrop;
   about 24 oz.)

2 Tbsp. olive oil

   Kosher salt and freshly ground
   black pepper

When you grill cherry tomatoes, they not only take on a live-fire char and smoky flavor, they collapse, becoming extra juicy and unbelievably sweet. You now have the perfect summery base for salads and sides that beg to be paired with other grilled foods. Turn the page for two recipes that use them.

Toss tomatoes with oil; season with salt and pepper. Put in a preheated grill basket and grill over high heat, turning basket occasionally, until tomatoes are charred and blistered, about 3 minutes. Remove from basket. Transfer to a plate to cool.

Our Favorite Cherry Tomatoes

Look beyond the little red guys in the plastic clamshell.

TEARDROP
Also called pear tomatoes, thanks to their curvy shape. Look for them in yellow, red, and vibrant orange varieties.

BLACK CHERRY
Available in brown and purplish hues, they're like the goths of the nightshade world.

SUN GOLD
Sweet and fruity, these tangerine dreams hold up well under fire.

GRILLED PANZANELLA

4 SERVINGS

1 bunch scallions

4 Tbsp. olive oil, divided, plus more for brushing

Kosher salt and freshly ground black pepper

4 slices thick country-style bread, crusts removed

1 garlic clove, halved

Grilled Cherry Tomatoes (see recipe, page 195)

2 cups arugula

2 Tbsp. red wine vinegar

For this riff on the classic Italian salad, grilling the bread dries it out a bit, so it can absorb more dressing. This is also a perfect way to use up day-old bread.

Toss scallions with 2 Tbsp. oil; season with salt and pepper. Grill over high heat, turning occasionally, until lightly charred, about 4 minutes. Let cool; coarsely chop.

Generously brush both sides of bread with oil; grill over high heat until golden brown, about 2 minutes per side. Rub with garlic and tear into pieces. Toss with scallions, grilled tomatoes, arugula, remaining 2 Tbsp. oil, and vinegar.

ISRAELI COUSCOUS and TOMATO SALAD

4 SERVINGS

1 cup Israeli couscous

2 Tbsp. olive oil, plus more for brushing

Grilled Cherry Tomatoes (see recipe, page 195)

½ head of radicchio

¼ small red onion, thinly sliced

Kosher salt and freshly ground black pepper

Shaved ricotta salata, chopped toasted almonds, fresh flat-leaf parsley leaves, and fresh oregano leaves (for serving)

Use any cooked grain or other small pasta for this summer favorite, in which the sweet tomatoes play off the bitter radicchio.

Cook Israeli couscous according to package directions; toss with 2 Tbsp. oil. Meanwhile, prepare grilled tomatoes.

Brush radicchio with oil; grill over high heat, turning occasionally, until lightly charred, 5–8 minutes. Let cool; coarsely chop. Toss with tomatoes, onion, and couscous; season with salt and pepper. Serve topped with ricotta, almonds, and parsley and oregano leaves.

ROASTED BEETS
WITH SESAME
AND MARJORAM
P. 200

SMASHED FINGERLINGS
WITH JALAPEÑOS
P. 201

ROASTED BEETS
with SESAME
and MARJORAM

8 SERVINGS

4 bunches of beets with tops
  or 2 lb. medium beets plus
  ½ bunch Swiss chard, ribs
  and stems removed, leaves
  torn into large pieces

5 Tbsp. olive oil, divided

  Kosher salt, freshly ground
  black pepper

½ bunch marjoram or oregano,
  plus 2 Tbsp. leaves

½ cup crème fraîche

½ cup plain whole-milk
  Greek yogurt

1 tsp. plus 1 Tbsp. Sherry vinegar
  or red wine vinegar

2 Tbsp. toasted sesame seeds

This Eastern Mediterranean–inspired side dish looks prettiest when not piled too high. If you're serving it family style, we recommend dividing it over two platters and putting one at each end of the table.

Preheat oven to 400°. Trim tops from beets; set aside half of tops (reserve remainder for another use). Scrub beets, pat dry, and slice ¼" thick. Toss in a large bowl with 4 Tbsp. oil; season with salt and pepper.

Scatter marjoram sprigs across a rimmed baking sheet and arrange beets on top in as even a layer as possible (some overlap is okay). Roast, tossing occasionally, until beets are tender, 15–20 minutes. Remove from oven and toss in reserved beet greens; roast just until slightly wilted, about 2 minutes. Let cool.

Meanwhile, whisk crème fraîche, yogurt, and 1 tsp. vinegar in a small bowl; season with salt; set aside.

Smash sesame seeds, 2 Tbsp. marjoram leaves, and a generous pinch of salt in a mortar and pestle to combine. (Alternatively, chop with a knife.) Transfer to a small bowl and mix in remaining 1 Tbsp. oil; set sesame salt aside.

Drizzle roasted beets and greens with remaining 1 Tbsp. vinegar; season with salt and pepper. Spoon reserved crème fraîche mixture between 2 platters and arrange beets and greens on top; sprinkle with sesame salt.

DO AHEAD: Beets (without greens) can be roasted 1 day ahead. Let cool; cover and chill. Bring to room temperature before using; sauté greens separately. Sesame salt can be made 2 days ahead; cover and chill.

*There's no real need to peel beets—
or carrots or Jerusalem artichokes,
for that matter. Instead, lightly
scrub with a vegetable brush or a new
scouring pad under running water.
The farm-fresh look adds visual appeal,
making any beet or carrot—or
Jerusalem artichoke—dish that much
more sophisticated.*

SMASHED FINGERLINGS with JALAPEÑOS

8 SERVINGS

3 lb. fingerling potatoes, halved crosswise if large

½ cup olive oil, divided

Kosher salt, freshly ground black pepper

¼ cup Sherry vinegar or red wine vinegar

1 Tbsp. whole grain mustard

1 jalapeño, thinly sliced into rounds, seeds removed if desired

¼ cup (lightly packed) torn flat-leaf parsley leaves

Hit the reset button on your potato salad: These spuds—from Austin, Texas, chefs Lou Lambert and Larry McGuire—are roasted, not boiled, and tossed with a mustardy vinaigrette and jalapeños while warm.

Preheat oven to 450°. Toss potatoes with ¼ cup oil on a rimmed baking sheet; season with salt and pepper. Roast, tossing once, until golden brown and tender, 30–35 minutes. Let cool slightly, then lightly flatten.

Meanwhile, whisk vinegar and mustard in a large bowl. Gradually whisk in remaining ¼ cup oil until emulsified; season with salt and pepper. Add potatoes, jalapeño, and parsley and toss; season with salt and pepper.

CRISPY SALT-and-VINEGAR POTATOES

4 SERVINGS

2 lb. baby Yukon Gold potatoes, halved, quartered if large

1 cup plus 2 Tbsp. distilled white vinegar

1 Tbsp. kosher salt, plus more

2 Tbsp. unsalted butter

Freshly ground black pepper

2 Tbsp. chopped fresh chives

Flaky sea salt (such as Maldon)

The addictive flavor of salt-and-vinegar potato chips dresses up for the dinner table. The tart taste is built up in two steps: Cooking the potatoes in vinegar seasons them from within, and a final drizzle boosts the flavor.

Combine potatoes, 1 cup vinegar, and 1 Tbsp. kosher salt in a medium saucepan; add water to cover by 1". Bring to a boil, reduce heat, and simmer until potatoes are tender, 20–25 minutes; drain and pat dry.

Heat butter in a large skillet over medium-high heat. Add potatoes; season with kosher salt and pepper. Cook, tossing occasionally, until golden brown and crisp, 8–10 minutes. Drizzle with remaining 2 Tbsp. vinegar. Serve topped with chives and sea salt.

We ask a lot of potatoes: They should be crispy on the outside, creamy within. Our secret? Boil them first (which gets them tender but does no favors for the skin), then brown them in a skillet with butter. This yields color, more flavor, and crackling skin. Who says you can't have it all?

above:
GRILLED ZUCCHINI
AND LEEKS WITH
WALNUTS AND HERBS
P. 207

left:
CHARRED AND RAW
CORN WITH
CHILE AND CHEESE
P. 206

CHARRED and RAW CORN with CHILE and CHEESE

4 SERVINGS

4 ears of corn, husked

1 large shallot, thinly sliced into rings

½ red chile (such as Holland or Fresno), with seeds, thinly sliced into rings

¼ cup fresh lime juice

Kosher salt, freshly ground black pepper

4 Tbsp. vegetable oil, divided

2 oz. fresh Cotija cheese or queso fresco, crumbled

¼ cup cilantro leaves with tender stems

All the flavors of a Mexican grilled corn on the cob, now in a convenient, tossed-together form. You might never go back to the three-napkin version.

Prepare grill for medium heat. Cut kernels from 1 corn cob and toss with shallot, chile, and lime juice in a large bowl; season with salt and pepper and set aside.

Brush remaining 3 ears of corn with 2 Tbsp. oil and grill, turning occasionally, until very tender and charred in spots, 10–12 minutes. Let cool.

Cut kernels from cobs and add to reserved corn mixture along with cheese, cilantro, and remaining 2 Tbsp. oil. Toss to combine; season with salt and pepper.

GRILLED ZUCCHINI and LEEKS with WALNUTS AND HERBS

4 SERVINGS

½ cup walnuts

1 garlic clove, finely grated

2 Tbsp. fresh lemon juice

5 Tbsp. olive oil, divided

Kosher salt, freshly ground black pepper

2 large leeks, white and pale-green parts only, halved lengthwise with some root attached

2 large zucchini (about 1 lb.), halved lengthwise

½ cup (lightly packed) fresh flat-leaf parsley leaves with tender stems

For this Provençal-accented dish, we like the texture of the leeks and zucchini when left al dente—if grilled too long, they'll both go floppy and the zucchini will release too much liquid.

Prepare grill for medium-high heat. Toast walnuts in a dry small skillet over medium heat, tossing often, until fragrant, about 5 minutes. Chop very coarsely. Toss warm walnuts with garlic, lemon juice, and 3 Tbsp. oil in a large bowl; season with salt and pepper.

Brush leeks and zucchini with remaining 2 Tbsp. oil; season with salt and pepper. Grill vegetables, turning often, until tender and charred in spots, 5–8 minutes for leeks, 8–10 minutes for zucchini.

Transfer vegetables to a cutting board. Trim roots from leeks and cut leeks and zucchini into bite-size pieces. Add vegetables and parsley to bowl with walnuts and toss to combine; season vegetables with salt, pepper, and more lemon juice, if desired.

Tips for Grilling Perfect Vegetables

BEFRIEND FAT

Oil will allow the produce to take on even color and also help round out the dish's flavor. Just don't use butter—it'll burn.

LIVE LARGE

Grill vegetables whole, or cut them into big, chunky pieces. You won't lose them through the grates, plus you'll get a nice char without overcooking.

MOVE IT, MOVE IT

Keep the vegetables moving while you grill so they brown all over (this means you need to stand by, tongs in hand, while they cook).

GRILL, THEN CHILL

No need to serve these salads piping hot. Cook the veg ahead and assemble the dishes later—they're both great at room temperature.

SAUTÉED COLLARD GREENS with CARAMELIZED MISO BUTTER

8 SERVINGS

2 Tbsp. white miso

2 Tbsp. mirin (sweet Japanese rice wine)

2 Tbsp. unseasoned rice vinegar

¼ cup (½ stick) unsalted butter, cut into pieces

3 Tbsp. vegetable oil

4 garlic cloves, crushed

Kosher salt

2 large bunches collard greens, ribs and stems removed, leaves torn into large pieces (about 8 cups)

Freshly ground black pepper

1 lemon, quartered

Flip the script on a winter vegetable that's usually stewed: Collards are great when briefly sautéed. Pair this with rich meats, like a porterhouse or roast turkey.

Heat miso in a large skillet over medium, stirring constantly, until it starts to caramelize and brown (it will be very dark), about 3 minutes. Add mirin and vinegar, scraping up any browned bits. Reduce heat to low and, stirring constantly, add butter one piece at a time; stir until emulsified. Transfer miso butter to a small bowl and set aside.

Wipe out skillet. Heat oil over medium and cook garlic, smashing with a spoon, until golden brown and broken into bits, about 4 minutes. Using a slotted spoon, transfer garlic to a small bowl; season with salt.

Working in batches, add collard greens to same skillet, tossing and letting them wilt slightly before adding more; season with salt and pepper. Cook, tossing occasionally, until all greens are wilted, bright green, and crisp-tender, about 5 minutes. Add half of reserved miso butter and toss to coat.

Transfer collard greens to a large serving bowl and drizzle with remaining miso butter. Top with reserved garlic and squeeze lemon over.

OLIVE OIL–
ROASTED LEEKS

4 SERVINGS

6 leeks (white and pale-green
   parts only)
½ cup olive oil
   Kosher salt

This ultra-simple recipe is a favorite of our editor in chief, Adam Rapoport. Preheating the pan helps the leeks take on some color; cooking at a lower temperature ensures they're fully tender. Serve them with pretty much anything. They're also delicious at room temperature.

Place a rimmed baking sheet in oven and preheat to 400°. Cut leeks in half lengthwise. Rinse well and pat completely dry. Toss with oil in a large bowl; season with salt.

Arrange leeks, cut side down, on hot baking sheet and cover loosely with foil. Reduce oven temperature to 300°. Bake until leeks are lightly browned on cut sides and very tender, about 1½ hours.

Uncover leeks and turn cut side up. Increase oven temperature to 400°; roast leeks until golden brown, 15–20 minutes. (Reserve the oil for making vinaigrettes or roasting vegetables. Let cool; cover and chill.)

DO AHEAD: Leeks can be baked 4 hours ahead. Let cool and cover.

Clean Those Leeks!

You might be tempted to skip washing them, but don't—within their folds, leeks trap an impressive amount of grit. Here's how to prepare both whole and sliced leeks for cooking.

WHOLE LEEKS:
Slice off the root end and the dark-green tops. Halve the leeks lengthwise. Splay the folds apart and rinse them under running water, letting the grit run out.

SLICED LEEKS:
Slice off the root end and dark-green tops. Halve the leeks lengthwise. Slice them thinly and swish them in a bowl of cool water. Let them sit undisturbed for 5–10 minutes so the grit falls to the bottom of the bowl. Gently scoop out the leeks with your hands.

BROCCOLINI-CHEDDAR GRATIN with RYE BREADCRUMBS

8 SERVINGS

¼ loaf seeded rye bread, torn into 1" pieces (about 2 cups)

4 dried chiles de árbol, divided

4 Tbsp. olive oil, divided

Kosher salt, freshly ground black pepper

1 lb. broccolini, larger stalks halved lengthwise

4 Tbsp. finely grated Parmesan, divided

4 oz. white cheddar, thinly sliced

If our daily staff tastings are any indicator, you will fight your own relatives for the bits of cheesy goodness stuck to the bottom of the pan. The spicy rye breadcrumbs are great on any gratin (or salad).

Pulse bread in a food processor until coarse crumbs form (make them about the size of chickpeas or smaller). You should have about 1½ cups. Transfer breadcrumbs to a small bowl. Add 2 chiles and 2 Tbsp. oil and toss to combine; season with salt and pepper.

Heat a medium skillet over medium heat and toast breadcrumb mixture, stirring often, until browned and crisp, about 5 minutes; remove from heat.

Preheat oven to 425°. Toss broccolini on a rimmed baking sheet with remaining 2 Tbsp. oil; season with salt and pepper. Roast, tossing occasionally, until tender and bright green, 5–8 minutes. Let cool slightly. Transfer broccolini to a medium bowl and toss with 2 Tbsp. Parmesan and remaining 2 chiles; season with salt and pepper.

Place half of broccolini in a 2-qt. baking dish and top with half of cheddar. Add remaining broccolini and finish with remaining cheddar. Scatter breadcrumbs over and sprinkle with remaining 2 Tbsp. Parmesan. Bake until breadcrumbs are browned and cheese is melted, 10–15 minutes.

DO AHEAD: Breadcrumbs can be made 2 days ahead; store tightly wrapped at room temperature. Gratin can be assembled 6 hours ahead; cover and chill. Bake just before serving.

7

desserts

SOUR CHERRY PIE

8 SERVINGS

CRUST

⅓ cup almond flour

¼ cup granulated sugar

1 tsp. kosher salt

2½ cups all-purpose flour, plus more for surface

1 cup (2 sticks) chilled unsalted butter, cut into pieces

2 large egg yolks

FILLING AND ASSEMBLY

All-purpose flour for surface

1 cup granulated sugar

1 Tbsp. finely grated lime zest

3 Tbsp. cornstarch

Pinch of kosher salt

3 lb. fresh sour cherries, pitted, or 6 cups frozen sour cherries

1 large egg, beaten to blend

Demerara sugar or granulated sugar (for sprinkling)

Trapped moisture equals soggy pastry. Cutting simple slits in the top crust is fine, but we love the way these circular cutouts look. It's easy: Use the point of a large pastry tip (about ¾" diameter) to punch out circles in the dough, leaving a 3" border. Be sure to allow a little space between them to avoid tears.

The ultimate, all-out, perfect cherry pie. Sour cherries have a much more complex flavor than Bing or Rainier, and adding almond flour to the pastry dough makes for a super-tender, toasty-looking crust.

CRUST

Pulse almond flour, granulated sugar, salt, and 2½ cups all-purpose flour in a food processor. Add butter and pulse until mixture resembles coarse cornmeal.

Whisk egg yolks and ¼ cup ice water in a small bowl and drizzle over flour mixture. Pulse, drizzling in more ice water as needed, until dough just comes together (a few dry spots are okay).

Gently knead dough on a lightly floured surface until no dry spots remain, about 1 minute. Divide dough in half and pat each piece into a disk; wrap in plastic. Chill at least 2 hours. **DO AHEAD:** Dough can be made 3 days ahead. Keep chilled.

FILLING AND ASSEMBLY

Preheat oven to 425°. Let dough sit at room temperature to soften slightly, about 5 minutes. Roll out 1 disk of dough on a lightly floured surface to a 12" round. Transfer to a parchment-lined baking sheet and chill. Repeat with remaining disk of dough.

Combine granulated sugar and lime zest in a large bowl, rubbing together with your fingertips to release oils in zest. Whisk in cornstarch and salt until there are no lumps in cornstarch. Add cherries and toss to coat.

Carefully transfer 1 crust to a 9" pie dish. Lift up edges and allow dough to slump down into dish. Trim edges to even out crust if needed. Scrape in cherry filling.

Using a ¾"-diameter pastry tip or cookie cutter, punch out holes in remaining crust, covering an area just smaller than the diameter of pie dish. Place over filling. Fold edge of top crust underneath edge of bottom crust and press together to seal. Crimp as desired. (Alternatively, assemble pie, then cut X's or slits into crust.) Brush crust with egg and sprinkle with demerara sugar. Chill pie until crust is firm, 20–30 minutes.

Place pie on a parchment- or foil-lined baking sheet. Bake until crust is golden, about 30 minutes. Reduce oven temperature to 350° and bake, tenting with foil if crust is browning too quickly, until juices are bubbling and crust is deep golden brown, 50–60 minutes longer. Transfer to a wire rack and let cool at least 4 hours before slicing. **DO AHEAD:** Pie can be baked 1 day ahead. Store tightly wrapped at room temperature.

BROWN BUTTER– POLENTA CAKE with MAPLE CARAMEL

10 SERVINGS

¾ cup (1½ sticks) unsalted butter, plus more for pan

¾ cup pure maple syrup

2 cups almond flour or meal

1 cup quick-cooking polenta

1½ tsp. baking powder

1 tsp. kosher salt

¾ cup plus 1 Tbsp. sugar

3 large eggs

½ cup heavy cream

½ cup sour cream

SPECIAL EQUIPMENT: A candy thermometer

For a cake so moist you won't believe it's gluten-free, be sure to use finely ground polenta labeled "quick-cooking" or "instant"; cooking times listed on the package will be five minutes or less.

Preheat oven to 350°. Butter a 9"-diameter cake pan and line bottom with a round of parchment paper; butter parchment.

Melt ¾ cup butter in a medium saucepan over medium heat, then cook, stirring often, until butter foams, then browns (do not let burn), 5–8 minutes. Pour into a medium bowl; let cool. Chill brown butter until cold.

Fit a clean medium saucepan with thermometer and bring maple syrup to a boil over medium-high heat; cook until thermometer registers 265° (syrup will be thicker and a shade darker). Pour into prepared pan and spread with an offset spatula or a spoon to cover bottom; let cool (syrup will harden as it sits).

Whisk almond flour, polenta, baking powder, and salt in a medium bowl. Using an electric mixer on medium-high speed, beat chilled brown butter and ¾ cup sugar until very pale and fluffy, 5–7 minutes. Add eggs 1 at a time, beating to blend between additions. Beat until light and fluffy, about 4 minutes. Reduce speed to low, gradually add dry ingredients, and mix just to combine. Scrape batter into pan; smooth top.

Bake until cake is golden brown and pulls away from sides of pan, 50–55 minutes. Transfer pan to a wire rack; let cake cool in pan 20 minutes. Turn out onto rack and let cool completely.

Using an electric mixer, beat heavy cream, sour cream, and remaining 1 Tbsp. sugar in a medium bowl until soft peaks form. Serve cake with whipped-cream mixture.

DO AHEAD: Cake can be baked 1 day ahead. Store tightly wrapped at room temperature.

PLUM TARTS with HONEY and BLACK PEPPER

6 SERVINGS

1 sheet frozen puff pastry (one 14-oz. package or half of 17.3-oz. package), thawed according to package directions

1 lb. red plums, apricots, or peaches, pitted, cut into ½" wedges

¼ cup sugar

Freshly ground black pepper

1 Tbsp. honey

Flaky sea salt (such as Maldon)

Consider this a two-ingredient tart. Besides the plums and pastry, we bet you have everything else on hand. This recipe will also work beautifully with peaches and nectarines.

Preheat oven to 425°. Cut pastry into six 4" squares, place on a parchment-lined baking sheet, and prick all over with a fork. Top with plums, leaving a ½" border. Sprinkle with sugar; season with a few grinds of pepper.

Bake tarts, rotating pan halfway through, until edges of pastry are puffed and golden brown, 25–30 minutes. Drizzle with honey and sprinkle with salt just before serving.

DO AHEAD: Tarts can be baked 4 hours ahead. Keep at room temperature.

Swap It!

Here are a few ways to switch up this tart. The combinations are endless (but always delicious).

FRUIT
Try berries in place of stone fruit. Come fall, sliced apples or pears make a fine stand-in (just don't forget the cinnamon!).

SWEETENER
Instead of white sugar, try demerara to add depth and a little texture. Or substitute maple syrup for the honey— it's especially nice with those apples.

HERBS AND SPICES
Swap toasted fennel seeds for the pepper (great with apricots), add a pinch of cardamom or grated fresh ginger to berries, or top peaches with chopped rosemary.

CHOCOLATE-CARAMEL PECAN TART

12 SERVINGS

2 cups pecans

Basic Tart Dough (see recipe, page 230)

All-purpose flour (for surface)

1¼ cups sugar

¼ cup light corn syrup

¼ cup heavy cream

2 Tbsp. bourbon (optional)

1 oz. bittersweet chocolate, coarsely chopped

2 Tbsp. unsalted butter, cut into pieces

1 tsp. kosher salt

Flaky sea salt (such as Maldon)

SPECIAL EQUIPMENT: A 10"-diameter tart pan with removable bottom

You can also bake this candy bar of a tart in an 8x8" pan, but whatever you do, toast those nuts. Not only does it intensify the flavor (especially important in a tart, when there's all that sugar and chocolate to compete with), but it also ensures maximum crunch. Try a 350-degree oven for 10 minutes, then cut one open to check if it's golden brown through and through.

Place a rack in middle of oven and preheat to 350°. Toast pecans on a rimmed baking sheet, tossing occasionally, until fragrant and darkened, 10–15 minutes (you want them well toasted). Let cool, then coarsely chop.

Roll out dough on a lightly floured surface into a 13" round. Transfer to pan. Lift up edge and allow dough to slump down into pan; trim excess. Prick dough in a few places with a fork to prevent bubbles. Cover with parchment paper or heavy-duty foil, leaving overhang. Fill with pie weights or dried beans.

Place pan on a rimmed baking sheet and bake until crust is just golden and dry around the edge, 10–15 minutes. Remove pie weights and parchment and bake until golden brown and surface looks dry, 10–15 minutes longer. Transfer pan to a wire rack and let crust cool.

Meanwhile, cook sugar and corn syrup in a medium pot over medium heat, stirring occasionally, until dark amber, 8–10 minutes. Remove from heat and, whisking, gradually add cream and bourbon, if using. Add chocolate, butter, and kosher salt, stirring until chocolate and butter are melted; stir in pecans. Scrape filling into crust; sprinkle with sea salt. Let sit at room temperature at least 1 hour before slicing.

DO AHEAD: Tart can be baked 3 days ahead. Store tightly wrapped at room temperature.

STRAWBERRY-BASIL SHORTCAKES

8 SERVINGS

SHORTCAKES

¼ cup sugar

1 Tbsp. baking powder

½ tsp. kosher salt

2 cups all-purpose flour,
   plus more for surface

6 Tbsp. (¾ stick) chilled unsalted
   butter, cut into pieces

1 cup heavy cream

1 large egg, beaten to blend

BERRIES AND ASSEMBLY

1½ lb. fresh strawberries,
   hulled, quartered
   (about 3 cups), divided

4 Tbsp. sugar, divided

2 sprigs basil

2 cups heavy cream

2 Tbsp. crème fraîche

We love the combination of gently cooked and raw strawberries in this not-too-sweet version of the classic dessert—from chef Chris Fischer of the Beach Plum Restaurant on Martha's Vineyard. Mint or tarragon would be nice in place of the basil.

SHORTCAKES

Preheat oven to 400°. Whisk sugar, baking powder, salt, and 2 cups flour in a large bowl. Using your fingers or a pastry cutter, work in butter until the texture of coarse meal with a few pea-size pieces of butter remaining. Add cream and mix until dough just comes together (it will be sticky).

Turn out dough onto a lightly floured surface and pat into a 12x4" rectangle about ¾" thick. Cut out rounds with a 2½" biscuit cutter, rerolling scraps as needed to make 8 rounds. Whisk egg with 1 Tbsp. water in a small bowl. Transfer rounds to a parchment-lined baking sheet and brush tops with egg wash. Bake until tops are golden brown and shortcakes are cooked through, 15–20 minutes.

DO AHEAD: Shortcakes can be made 2 days ahead. Store tightly wrapped at room temperature.

BERRIES AND ASSEMBLY

Coarsely chop 2 cups strawberries (use any bruised or less perfect ones) and cook with 2 Tbsp. sugar in a medium saucepan over medium heat, stirring occasionally, until berries are softened and mixture is slightly thickened, about 5 minutes. Let berry compote cool.

Meanwhile, toss basil, 1 Tbsp. sugar, and remaining 1 cup strawberries in a medium bowl and let sit until fruit begins to release juices, 10–15 minutes. Discard basil.

Using an electric mixer, beat cream, crème fraîche, and remaining 1 Tbsp. sugar to soft peaks, about 4 minutes.

Split shortcakes and fill with berry compote, whipped cream mixture, and macerated strawberries.

CHOCOLATE-COCONUT POUND CAKE

8 SERVINGS

¼ cup unsalted butter, plus more

1½ cups all-purpose flour

½ cup unsweetened cocoa powder

1 tsp. kosher salt

¾ tsp. baking powder

½ cup virgin coconut oil, room temperature

1½ cups plus 1 Tbsp. sugar

3 large eggs

1 tsp. vanilla extract

⅔ cup buttermilk

¼ cup unsweetened coconut flakes

The fragrant richness of coconut oil and the tenderizing power of buttermilk make this moist pound cake a crowd-pleaser.

Preheat oven to 325°. Butter an 8x4" loaf pan; line with parchment paper, leaving a generous overhang on long sides. Whisk flour, cocoa powder, salt, and baking powder in a medium bowl; set aside.

Using an electric mixer on medium-high speed, beat oil, ¼ cup butter, and 1½ cups sugar until pale and fluffy, 5–7 minutes. Add eggs one at a time, beating to blend between additions; beat until mixture is very light and doubled in volume, 5–8 minutes. Add vanilla.

Reduce mixer speed to low and add dry ingredients in 3 additions, alternating with buttermilk in 2 additions, beginning and ending with dry ingredients (do not overmix; it will cause cake to buckle and split). Scrape batter into prepared pan and run a spatula through the center, creating a canal. Sprinkle with coconut and remaining 1 Tbsp. sugar.

Bake cake, tenting with foil if coconut browns too much before cake is done (it should be very dark and toasted), until a tester inserted into the center comes out clean, 70–80 minutes. Transfer pan to a wire rack; let cake cool in pan 20 minutes before turning out.

DO AHEAD: Cake can be baked 5 days ahead. Keep tightly wrapped at room temperature.

Just Call It *Bettermilk*

Everything you need to know about buttermilk, our favorite "new" old-fashioned ingredient.

REAL BUTTERMILK

Old-fashioned buttermilk is what's left after cream has been churned into butter. Naturally low-fat, it looks like thick milk. (Cultures are added to thicken it further.) Look for bottles from local dairies at specialty shops or the farmers' market.

SUPERMARKET STANDARD

Most buttermilk in the dairy aisle starts with low-fat milk and isn't derived from butter. It's interchangeable with traditional buttermilk (hence perfectly suitable for baking), though it lacks the rich flavor and tartness of the real thing.

BEYOND BAKING

Use any extra buttermilk to make Indian *lassis* or add it to fruit smoothies, stir a little into oatmeal for some creaminess, brine chicken in it, or mix it with yogurt, scallions, and lemon zest to make a quick savory dip.

SALTED-BUTTER APPLE GALETTE with MAPLE WHIPPED CREAM

8 SERVINGS

¼ cup (½ stick) salted butter

½ vanilla bean, split lengthwise

Basic Tart Dough (see recipe, page 230)

All-purpose flour (for dusting)

1 lb. baking apples (such as Pink Lady; about 2 large), scrubbed, sliced ⅛" thick

3 Tbsp. dark muscovado or dark brown sugar

1 large egg

1 Tbsp. granulated sugar

2 cups heavy cream

2 Tbsp. pure maple syrup

This laid-back apple galette got a standing ovation during tastings in the *BA* Test Kitchen, thanks to its crisp yet tender crust and the ideal sweet-salty balance.

Place a rack in middle of oven and preheat to 375°. Place butter in a small saucepan and scrape in vanilla seeds; add pod. Cook over medium heat, stirring often, until butter foams, then browns (be careful not to burn), 5–8 minutes. Remove pan from heat and remove pod.

Roll out dough on a lightly floured surface into a rough 14x10" overlapping and leaving rectangle about ⅛" thick (alternatively, roll out into a 12" round). Transfer to a parchment-lined baking sheet. Arrange apples on top, overlapping and leaving a 1½" border. Brush apples with brown butter and sprinkle with muscovado sugar. Lift edges of dough over apples, tucking and overlapping as needed to keep rectangular shape.

Beat egg with 1 tsp. water in a small bowl and brush crust with egg wash. Sprinkle with granulated sugar and bake, rotating once, until apples are soft and juicy and crust is golden brown, 40–50 minutes. Let cool slightly on baking sheet before slicing.

Beat cream in a medium bowl to medium-soft peaks. Fold in maple syrup and serve alongside galette.

DO AHEAD: Galette can be baked 2 days ahead. Store tightly wrapped at room temperature. Reheat slightly before serving.

BASIC TART DOUGH

*MAKES ENOUGH FOR ONE 10"-DIAMETER TART
OR ONE 14X10" GALETTE*

1 Tbsp. sugar

½ tsp. kosher salt

1 cup all-purpose flour, plus
more for surface

6 Tbsp. chilled unsalted butter,
cut into pieces

1 large egg, beaten to blend

Too-cold doughs can crack and split when rolled; let this sit at room temperature for five minutes after removing from the fridge. And remember: Those uneven edges are part of the apple galette's charm.

Whisk sugar, salt, and 1 cup flour in a medium bowl. Add butter and rub in with your fingers until mixture resembles coarse meal with a few pea-size pieces remaining. Drizzle egg over butter mixture and mix gently with a fork until dough just comes together.

Turn out dough onto a lightly floured surface and knead until smooth (a few dry spots are okay). Form dough into a disk. Wrap in plastic and chill until firm, at least 2 hours.

DO AHEAD: Dough can be made 2 days ahead. Keep chilled, or freeze up to 1 month.

A Grand Galette

Walk the line between rustic and showstopping with your new star dessert. Here's how to ace it.

1
CORE
Cut apples off the core into three lobes. This not only neatly gets rid of the core, it also gives you flat pieces, which make for easier slicing. And you can snack on what's left.

2
SLICE
Cut each section into slices about ⅛" thick. (Use a sharp knife or you'll bruise the flesh.) As you cut, make sure you hold the section together—it helps with step 4.

3
ROLL
Roll out dough on a lightly floured work surface into a rectangle about 14x10". Don't worry if the edges are uneven; they'll give the galette a pretty, homemade character.

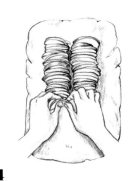

4
ARRANGE
Transfer apple slices to prepared dough, fanning them out so they lie flatter (they can be as perfect or imperfect as you like). Make sure to leave a 2" border of dough.

5
SPRINKLE
Brush the tops of the fanned-out apples with nutty brown butter, then sprinkle with muscovado sugar for extra richness and depth with a delightfully sweet crunch.

6
FOLD
Starting at one edge, fold dough onto apples. Work around each side, overlapping as needed. Brush outside edge with egg wash and sprinkle with granulated sugar.

NUTTY GRAIN and OAT BARS

MAKES ABOUT 16

Nonstick vegetable oil spray

6 large Medjool dates, pitted, chopped

1 cup pure maple syrup

2 Tbsp. unsalted butter or virgin coconut oil

2 cups old-fashioned oats

½ cup raw almonds, hazelnuts, pecans, walnuts, or cashews

½ cup shelled pumpkin seeds (pepitas)

½ cup shelled sunflower seeds

2 Tbsp. amaranth

½ tsp. kosher salt

* **ALSO TRY IT WITH:** Sesame seeds instead of amaranth

This crunchy, nutty, oat-packed loaf can be sliced for breakfast on the go, toasted and topped with yogurt or cream cheese, or eaten in place of an energy bar.

Preheat oven to 350°. Lightly coat an 8½x4" loaf pan with nonstick spray and line with parchment paper, leaving an overhang on long sides; spray parchment.

Bring dates and maple syrup to a boil in a small saucepan, reduce heat to medium-high, and boil, stirring often, until dates are very soft and maple syrup is slightly reduced, 8–10 minutes. Remove date mixture from heat and stir in butter until it is melted. Mash dates with a potato masher or fork until as smooth as possible (if you have an immersion blender, it will work, too). You should have about 1 cup.

Toss oats, almonds, pumpkin seeds, sunflower seeds, amaranth, and salt in a large bowl. Mix in date mixture until evenly coated. Scrape half of oat mixture into prepared pan and press very firmly and evenly with a rubber spatula to compress it as much as possible. Add remaining oat mixture and press until very tightly packed into pan.

Bake, tenting with foil if browning too quickly, until loaf is darkened in color and firm around the edges, and center gives just slightly when pressed, 45–50 minutes. Transfer pan to a wire rack and let loaf cool in pan before turning out (it can even sit overnight). Cut into ½"-thick slices with a serrated knife.

For crisp bars, lay slices on a baking sheet and bake at 350° until golden brown, 8–10 minutes, or toast as desired in a toaster oven.

DO AHEAD: Loaf can be made 5 days ahead. Keep tightly wrapped at room temperature.

We can't stress it enough: Pack the mixture as tightly as possible into the loaf pan. This is essential for the slices to hold together when cut.

SALTED PEANUT BUTTER and JELLY BLONDIES

MAKES 16

½ cup (1 stick) unsalted butter, melted, plus more for pan

1¼ cups all-purpose flour

1 tsp. baking powder

1 tsp. kosher salt

2 large eggs

1½ cups light brown sugar

¾ cup smooth peanut butter

1 tsp. vanilla extract

2 Tbsp. strawberry jam

1 Tbsp. chopped honey-roasted peanuts

Flaky sea salt (such as Maldon)

These are really peanut-buttery and not too sweet, so the jam on top is a perfect complement.

Preheat oven to 350°. Butter an 8x8" baking pan. Whisk together flour, baking powder, and salt. Whisk together eggs, brown sugar, peanut butter, melted butter, and vanilla; fold in dry ingredients. Scrape batter into prepared pan. Dollop with strawberry jam; top with peanuts.
Bake until a tester comes out clean, 35–40 minutes. Sprinkle with flaky sea salt.

MATCHA–WHITE CHOCOLATE SUGAR COOKIES

MAKES 24

¾ cup granulated sugar, divided

½ tsp. plus 2 Tbsp. matcha

2 cups all-purpose flour

¾ tsp. baking soda

½ tsp. kosher salt

1 cup (2 sticks) plus 2 Tbsp. unsalted butter, cut into pieces, room temperature

½ cup (packed) light brown sugar

1½ Tbsp. honey

1 large egg

1 large egg yolk

2 tsp. finely grated lemon zest

3 oz. white chocolate, chopped

INGREDIENT INFO: Matcha, also called green tea powder, is available at Japanese markets and some supermarkets, and online.

Powdered green tea gives these tender cookies from Craftsman and Wolves in San Francisco an elf-worthy hue that will stand out. Also try adding a little chopped candied ginger or dried apricots.

Whisk ½ cup granulated sugar and ½ tsp. matcha in a bowl; set aside.

Whisk flour, baking soda, salt, and remaining 2 Tbsp. matcha in a medium bowl. Using an electric mixer on medium-high speed, beat butter, brown sugar, honey, and remaining ¼ cup granulated sugar in a medium bowl until light and fluffy, about 4 minutes. Add egg, egg yolk, and lemon zest and mix until very pale, about 4 minutes.

Reduce mixer speed to low and, with motor running, add flour mixture; mix until no dry spots remain. Using a wooden spoon or rubber spatula, mix in white chocolate.

Wrap dough in plastic and chill at least 2 hours and up to 5 days. If chilling more than a few hours, let dough sit at room temperature 1 hour to soften before scooping and baking.

Preheat oven to 350°. Scoop the dough by the scant tablespoonful onto 2 parchment-lined baking sheets, spacing about 1" apart. (Or, for neat and tidy cookies with perfect edges, like the ones in our photo, portion same amount of dough into the cups of a mini muffin pan coated with nonstick vegetable oil spray.)

Bake cookies, rotating baking sheet halfway through, until bottoms and edges are barely golden and top no longer looks wet, 8–10 minutes.

Immediately—but gently—toss cookies in reserved matcha sugar and place on wire racks; let cool.

DO AHEAD: Store cookies airtight at room temperature up to 2 days.

Matcha Made in Heaven

What to do with the rest of that matcha? Here are three steps to foamy, green-mustachioed perfection:

1

MEASURE

Place ¼ tsp. matcha into a small bowl and use a whisk to gently break up clumps.

2

POUR

Slowly pour ⅓ cup of not-quite-boiling water into the center of the bowl. (You can also use milk or your alt-milk of choice.)

3

FROTH

Whisk briskly in an up-and-down motion (like writing the letters M and W) until the tea is frothy, 15–20 seconds.

LAVENDER
SHORTBREAD
WITH FRUITS,
FLOWERS,
AND HERBS
P. 240

LAVENDER SHORTBREAD
with FRUITS, FLOWERS, and HERBS

MAKES 20

Upgrade from those Technicolor sugars in the back of the cupboard. Vibrant toppers like edible dried flowers, festive candied herbs, and colorful freeze-dried fruits dress up any holiday cookie—especially this lavender shortbread from San Francisco's Craftsman and Wolves. They're easy to find in the baking or tea aisles of well-stocked supermarkets.

GLAZE

3 large egg whites

4 cups powdered sugar

½ tsp. cream of tartar

SHORTBREAD AND ASSEMBLY

⅓ cup rice flour

1½ tsp. kosher salt

2½ cups all-purpose flour, plus more

1 cup plus 6 Tbsp. unsalted butter, cut into pieces, room temperature

¾ cup granulated sugar

1 tsp. coarsely ground dried lavender

Freeze-dried and/or dried fruits, dried edible flowers, fresh and/or dried herbs (for decorating)

SPECIAL EQUIPMENT: One 3⅛"-diameter and one 1¼"-diameter fluted cutter

GLAZE

Using a wooden spoon or rubber spatula, stir egg whites, powdered sugar, and cream of tartar in a medium bowl until a thick paste forms with no dry spots. Ideally, glaze should sit at least 12 hours for sugar to fully hydrate, but it can be used as soon as cookies have cooled. Or, you can cover and chill up to 1 week. Bring to room temperature before using.

SHORTBREAD AND ASSEMBLY

Whisk rice flour, salt, and 2½ cups all-purpose flour in a medium bowl. Using an electric mixer on medium-high, beat butter, sugar, and lavender in a medium bowl until very pale and fluffy, about 5 minutes. Mix in dry ingredients on low until fully combined. Wrap in plastic and chill at least 2 hours and up to 2 days.

Preheat oven to 350°. Roll out dough between 2 sheets of lightly floured parchment to ⅛" thick. Using large cutter, cut out 16 rounds, rerolling scraps. Using small cutter, punch out centers. Bake on parchment-lined baking sheets until edges are golden, 12–14 minutes. Let cool on a wire rack.

Working quickly, dip tops of cookies into glaze, letting excess drip off. Transfer to wire rack and decorate.

DO AHEAD: Store shortbread airtight at room temperature up to 1 week.

How to Become a Wreath Expert

These deceptively simple lavender shortbread wreaths will rule your next cookie swap.
See below for how to pull them off, or watch our video at bonappetit.com/holidays.

1

ROLL

Roll out the cookie dough between two sheets of lightly floured parchment paper until it's about ⅛" thick.

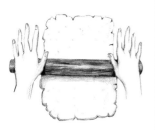

2

CUT

Using two round cutters (one smaller than the other to make the wreath's center), punch out circle, then cut out center.

3

GLAZE

Dip baked cookies into the glaze and let the excess drip back into the bowl. Try two or three at a time, then go immediately to step 4.

4

DECORATE

Adorn these cookies however you please, just work quickly—the toppings won't stick to dry glaze. You've got a minute or so to go wild.

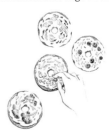

CHOCOLATE BROWNIE COOKIES

MAKES 2 DOZEN

3 cups gluten-free powdered sugar

¾ cup unsweetened cocoa powder

1 tsp. kosher salt

2 large egg whites

1 large egg

4 oz. bittersweet chocolate, chopped

3 Tbsp. cacao nibs

If a fudgy brownie and chewy chocolate chip cookie had a baby, it would be this decadent (and gluten-free) creation. The cooling time is key. There is a sweet spot: Ideally you want to eat these warm, but too warm and they'll fall apart.

Place racks in lower and upper thirds of oven; preheat to 350°. Whisk powdered sugar, cocoa powder, and salt in a large bowl, then whisk in egg whites and egg; fold in chocolate and cacao nibs. Spoon batter by the tablespoonful onto 2 parchment-lined baking sheets, spacing 2" apart.

Bake, rotating sheets once, until cookies are puffed, cracked, and set just around the edges, 14–16 minutes.

Transfer baking sheets to wire racks and let cookies cool on pan (they'll firm up).

DO AHEAD: Cookies can be baked 3 days ahead. Store airtight at room temperature.

Know Your Chocolate

Chocolate may be universally loved, but working with it can be confusing. (Dark? Bittersweet? Milk?) We asked Mast Brothers' director of chocolate, Vesa Parviainen, to break down some common terms and ingredients.

CACAO

The name of the tree that produces the beans that are the base of chocolate. Cacao beans are transformed by fermentation and dried before processing. Each bean contains a rich nib (see below) and a thin shell called a husk. Note: *Cacao* and *cocoa* can be used interchangeably, but generally *cocoa* is used to describe processed cacao products.

COCOA NIBS

The foundation of chocolate, these have the look and crumbly consistency of roasted coffee beans (and make a great dessert garnish). All those good things about chocolate—antioxidants, vitamins, and yes, caffeine—are in here.

COCOA POWDER

This is essentially what's left of the nibs after they've been ground and pressed. Natural cocoa powder is intense in flavor but lighter in color. Dutch-process cocoa powder has been alkalized, mellowing the flavor and darkening the color. Unless a recipe specifies, you can use either type.

DARK CHOCOLATE

A generic term used for chocolate with no added milk solids (sugar, however, is okay). Dark chocolate—including bars labeled semisweet, bittersweet, and unsweetened—can contain anywhere from 35 to 80 percent cacao.

MILK CHOCOLATE

This is the sweet, mellow chocolate most Americans grew up on (hello, Hershey's!). Milk solids are used to tweak both the flavor profile and mouthfeel.

WHITE CHOCOLATE

Not technically chocolate because it doesn't contain any cocoa particles, this ivory-colored confection is made with cocoa butter, sugar, and milk solids.

ANISEED-ALMOND MERINGUES

MAKES 16

1   Tbsp. aniseed plus more

4   large egg whites

⅔   cup granulated sugar

¾   cup powdered sugar

½   cup sliced skin-on almonds

Love to eat Good & Plentys? These featherweight, licoricey meringues from Måurice Luncheonette in Portland, Oregon—one of our Best New Restaurants of 2014—are for you.

Preheat oven to 200°. Toast aniseed in a dry small skillet over medium heat, tossing often, until fragrant, about 2 minutes; let cool. Using an electric mixer on high speed, beat egg whites until frothy, about 1 minute.

With motor running, gradually add granulated sugar and beat until medium peaks form, 8–10 minutes. Then gradually add powdered sugar and beat until stiff peaks form, about 5 minutes longer. Fold in aniseed.

Spoon meringue onto a parchment-lined baking sheet, top with almonds and more aniseed, and bake until dry, 2–2½ hours. Turn off heat and let cool in oven.

Resist the urge to crank up the oven! The key to perfectly crisp, snow-white meringues is to let them slowly dry out in a low-temperature oven.

NANA'S BUTTER COOKIES with MILK-JAM FILLING

MAKES 16

COOKIES

1½ cups (3 sticks) unsalted butter, room temperature

⅔ cup powdered sugar

2 tsp. vanilla extract

2 Tbsp. whole milk

2 tsp. kosher salt

2½ cups all-purpose flour, plus more

1 large egg

MILK JAM AND ASSEMBLY

1 qt. goat's milk or cow's milk

1¼ cups granulated sugar

¾ tsp. baking soda

½ vanilla bean, halved lengthwise

Powdered sugar (optional; for serving)

These aren't the cookies to underbake, says Kristen Murray of Mâurice in Portland, Oregon—one of our Best New Restaurants of 2014. If they're not browned enough after 15 minutes, keep them in the oven for a few more. What they gain in color, they gain in deep, nutty flavor, too. They're excellent on their own, just in case you want to skip the milk-jam filling.

COOKIES

Using an electric mixer on high speed, beat butter, powdered sugar, and vanilla in a medium bowl until light and fluffy, about 4 minutes. Reduce speed to low; add milk, salt, and 2½ cups flour and mix just to combine. Form dough into a ½"-thick disk and wrap in plastic. Chill until firm, at least 1 hour.

Let dough sit at room temperature to soften slightly, about 5 minutes. Roll dough out between 2 sheets of parchment paper until about ⅛" thick. Cut out rounds with a floured 2½"-diameter cookie cutter. Cut out a circle in half of the rounds with a ¾"-diameter cookie cutter and transfer to 2 parchment-lined baking sheets, spacing 1" apart.

Whisk egg and 1 tsp. water in a small bowl and brush tops of cookies with egg wash. Bake cookies, rotating halfway through, until golden brown, 12–15 minutes. Transfer baking sheets to wire racks and let cookies cool.

DO AHEAD: Dough can be made 5 days ahead. Keep chilled.

MILK JAM AND ASSEMBLY

Combine milk, sugar, and baking soda in a large saucepan; scrape in vanilla seeds and add pod. Bring just to a boil over medium heat, stirring to dissolve sugar. Reduce heat and simmer, whisking occasionally, until mixture is reduced to about 1¼ cups (it will darken and separate, with little bits visible), 80–90 minutes. Strain milk jam through a fine-mesh sieve into a medium bowl and let cool.

Spoon a small amount of milk jam onto flat side of a cookie without a hole and sandwich with a cookie with a hole. Repeat with remaining cookies and filling. Dust with powdered sugar, if desired.

DO AHEAD: Milk jam can be made 1 week ahead. Cover and chill.

TAHINI COOKIES

MAKES ABOUT 15

1 cup all-purpose flour

½ cup toasted pine nuts

⅓ cup powdered sugar

⅓ cup tahini

¼ cup unsalted butter (½ stick), room temperature

½ tsp. kosher salt

2 Tbsp. black sesame seeds

2 Tbsp. demerara sugar

The creamy sesame seed paste isn't just for hummus: It's the secret ingredient in this effortless confection. Got kids in the house? Let them do the rolling and flattening.

Preheat oven to 350°. Pulse flour, pine nuts, powdered sugar, tahini, butter, and salt in a food processor until dough forms a ball around blade.

Mix black sesame seeds and demerara sugar in a small bowl. Form dough into 1" balls and roll in sesame seed mixture. Place on a parchment-lined rimmed baking sheet, spacing 2" apart, and flatten slightly. Bake cookies until lightly golden, 20–25 minutes.

Three things to know about tahini:
1. We prefer roasted tahini to
raw: Roasting brings out the sweetness
and depth of the sesame seeds.
2. It separates; stir with a fork
to reincorporate the oil. 3. Some brands
can be bitter. We like Joyva best.

STRAWBERRY, POMEGRANATE, and ROSE PETAL MESS

6 SERVINGS

MERINGUES
- 2 large egg whites
- ¼ cup granulated sugar
- ¼ cup powdered sugar

ASSEMBLY
- ¾ cup crème fraîche
- ½ cup mascarpone
- 2 Tbsp. powdered sugar
- ½ tsp. rose water (optional)
- 6 oz. strawberries, hulled, halved if large
- 1 pint strawberry or raspberry sorbet
- 1 Tbsp. pomegranate molasses or 1½ tsp. honey
- ¼ cup pomegranate seeds
- 1 tsp. ground sumac
- 2 tsp. dried rose petals (optional)

INGREDIENT INFO: Sumac is available at specialty foods stores, and pomegranate molasses is available at some grocery stores. Both are available at Middle Eastern markets.

For this recipe by London chef Yotam Ottolenghi, you have our blessing to use store-bought meringues and skip the first step, if you prefer. But the quality of the berries is key, and you could add blackberries or raspberries if they look good at the market.

MERINGUES
Preheat oven to 200°. Using an electric mixer on medium-high speed, beat egg whites until foamy, about 1 minute. With mixer running, gradually add granulated sugar. Continue to beat until meringue triples in volume, is shiny, and holds medium-stiff peaks, 8–10 minutes. Add powdered sugar and beat just to blend.

Spoon 2 heaping tablespoonfuls of meringue onto a parchment-lined baking sheet; repeat to fill baking sheet, spacing 1" apart. Bake until dry, about 4 hours.

DO AHEAD: Meringues can be baked 5 days ahead. Keep airtight at room temperature.

ASSEMBLY
Whisk crème fraîche, mascarpone, powdered sugar, and rose water, if using, in a medium bowl.

Arrange meringues, crème fraîche mixture, strawberries, and scoops of sorbet in a large bowl. Drizzle with pomegranate molasses and top with pomegranate seeds, sumac, and rose petals, if using.

To seed a pomegranate, halve it, hold it cut side down over a bowl, and then whack the skin with a wooden spoon.

BLACKBERRY-TARRAGON PALETAS

MAKES 8

1½ pints blackberries

1 cup simple syrup

¼ cup fresh lemon juice

2 Tbsp. fresh tarragon leaves

Why do we love Mexican ice pops? Let us count the ways: They're perfectly cool on a sweltering day; they're surprisingly easy to throw together; they highlight the season's very best produce because they're made with puréed fresh fruit, and—best of all—they make people's eyes light up when you serve them. (You're just going to have to trust us on that last one.) Here are three of our favorite combos.

Purée blackberries, simple syrup, lemon juice, and tarragon until smooth. Strain through a fine-mesh sieve into a large measuring cup, divide among ice-pop molds, insert sticks, and freeze until solid, at least 6 hours.

RASPBERRY-MELON PALETAS

MAKES 8

3 lb. cantaloupe

½ pint fresh raspberries

1 cup simple syrup

2 Tbsp. fresh lemon juice

2 Tbsp. unseasoned rice vinegar

Remove skin and seeds from half of a 3-lb. cantaloupe. Purée flesh with raspberries, simple syrup, lemon juice, and vinegar until smooth.

Strain through a fine-mesh sieve into a large measuring cup, divide among ice-pop molds, insert sticks, and freeze until solid, at least 6 hours.

CUCUMBER-LIME PALETAS

MAKES 8

1 large cucumber (10–12 oz.), peeled

1 cup simple syrup

⅓ cup fresh lime juice

1 tsp. finely grated peeled ginger

Purée cucumber with simple syrup, lime juice, and ginger until smooth. Strain through a fine-mesh sieve into a large measuring cup, divide among ice-pop molds, insert sticks, and freeze until solid, at least 6 hours.

FROZEN YOGURT
with POACHED PEACHES

8 SERVINGS

FROZEN YOGURT

1 cup heavy cream

1 cup plain whole-milk Greek yogurt

1 cup whole milk

½ cup honey

2 Tbsp. fresh lemon juice

Pinch of kosher salt

PEACHES AND ASSEMBLY

4 large ripe peaches (about 2 lb.)

6 fresh lemon verbena leaves

1½ cups Cocchi Aperitivo Americano (Italian aperitif wine)

½ cup sugar

¼ cup chopped unsalted, raw pistachios

If you don't have an ice cream maker, use store-bought frozen yogurt, or serve the poached peaches over lightly sweetened Greek yogurt.

FROZEN YOGURT

Whisk cream, yogurt, milk, honey, lemon juice, and salt in a large bowl. Process in an ice cream maker according to manufacturer's instructions. Transfer frozen yogurt to an airtight container or a shallow baking pan; cover and freeze until firm, at least 2 hours.

DO AHEAD: Frozen yogurt can be made 1 week ahead. Keep frozen.

PEACHES AND ASSEMBLY

Using the tip of a paring knife, score an X in the bottom of each peach. Cook in a large pot of boiling water just until skins begin to peel back where cut, about 1 minute. Using a slotted spoon, transfer to a large bowl of ice water and let cool. Carefully peel peaches, reserving skins.

Bring lemon verbena, Cocchi Americano, sugar, reserved peach skins, and 1½ cups water to a boil in a medium saucepan. Reduce heat and simmer until mixture has thickened slightly and looks syrupy, 10–12 minutes.

Add peaches, cover saucepan, reduce heat, and gently poach fruit until the tip of a paring knife easily slides through flesh, 12–15 minutes. (Very ripe fruit will take less time to cook.) Using a slotted spoon, transfer peaches to a plate and let cool. Cut into wedges.

Meanwhile, return poaching liquid to a boil and cook until reduced by half, 15–20 minutes. Let cool, then discard solids.

Scoop frozen yogurt into small glasses or bowls and serve topped with peaches, some reduced poaching syrup, and pistachios.

DO AHEAD: Peaches can be poached 3 days ahead. Cover and chill in poaching liquid. Bring peaches to room temperature and reduce poaching liquid just before using.

KOUIGN-AMANN
P. 258

KOUIGN-AMANN

MAKES 12

DOUGH

- 2 Tbsp. (30 g) European-style butter (at least 82% fat), melted, slightly cooled, plus more for bowl
- 1 Tbsp. (10 g) active dry yeast
- 3 Tbsp. (40 g) sugar
- 1 tsp. (5 g) kosher salt
- 3 cups (400 g) all-purpose flour plus more for surface

BUTTER BLOCK

- 12 oz. (340 g) chilled unsalted European-style butter (at least 82% fat), cut into pieces
- ½ cup (100 g) sugar
- 1 tsp. (5 g) kosher salt

ASSEMBLY

- All-purpose flour
- ¾ cup (150 g) sugar, divided
- Nonstick vegetable oil spray

SPECIAL EQUIPMENT: Two 6-cup jumbo muffin pans; ruler

Picture a sugary, caramelized croissant and you'll see the wonders of this Breton classic. B. Patisserie's Belinda Leong taught us the secrets of the French pastry du jour. Though the dough can be temperamental, layer after delicate layer will convince you: Making this pastry is worth the effort. Turn the page for step-by-step photos.

DOUGH

Brush a large bowl with butter. Whisk yeast and ¼ cup very warm water (110°–115°) in another large bowl to dissolve. Let stand until yeast starts to foam, about 5 minutes. Add sugar, salt, 3 cups flour, 2 Tbsp. butter, and ¾ cup cold water. Mix until a shaggy dough forms. Turn out onto a lightly floured surface and knead, adding flour as needed, until dough is supple, soft, and slightly tacky, about 5 minutes.

Place dough in prepared bowl and turn to coat with butter. Cover bowl with plastic wrap, place in a warm, draft-free spot, and let dough rise until doubled in size, 1–1½ hours. (This process of resting and rising is known as proofing.) Punch down dough and knead lightly a few times inside bowl. Cover again with plastic wrap and chill in refrigerator until dough is again doubled in size, 45–60 minutes.

Turn out dough onto a lightly floured surface and pat into a 6x6" square. Wrap in plastic and chill in freezer until dough is very firm but not frozen, 30–35 minutes. (Heads up: You'll want it to be about as firm as the chilled butter block.)

BUTTER BLOCK

Beat butter, sugar, and salt with an electric mixer on low speed just until homogeneous and waxy-looking, about 3 minutes. Scrape butter mixture onto a large sheet of parchment. Shape into a 12x6" rectangle ¼" thick.

Neatly wrap up butter, pressing out air. Roll packet gently with a rolling pin to push butter into corners and create an evenly thick rectangle. Chill in refrigerator until firm but pliable, 25–30 minutes.

ASSEMBLY

Roll out dough on a lightly floured surface into a 19x7" rectangle (a bit wider and about 50 percent longer than the butter block). Place butter block on upper two-thirds of dough, leaving a thin border along top and sides. Fold dough like a letter: Bring lower third of dough up and over lower half of butter. Then fold exposed upper half of butter and dough over lower half (butter should bend, not break). Press edges of dough to seal, enclosing butter.

Rotate dough package 90° counterclockwise so flap opening is on your right. Roll out dough, dusting with flour as needed, to a 24x8" rectangle about ⅜" thick. Fold rectangle into thirds like a letter (same as before), bringing lower third up, then upper third down (this completes the first turn).

Dust dough lightly with flour, wrap in plastic, and chill in freezer until firm but not frozen, about 30 minutes. Transfer to refrigerator; continue to chill until very firm, about 1 hour longer. (Freezing dough first cuts down on chilling time.)

Place dough on surface so flap opening is on your right. Roll out dough, dusting with flour as needed, to a 24x8" rectangle, about ⅜" thick. Fold into thirds (same way as before), rotate 90° counterclockwise so flap opening is on your right, and roll out again to a 24x8" rectangle.

Sprinkle surface of dough with 2 Tbsp. sugar; fold into thirds. Dust lightly with flour, wrap in plastic, and chill in freezer until firm but not frozen, about 30 minutes. Transfer to refrigerator; continue to chill until very firm, about 1 hour longer.

Place dough on surface so flap opening is on your right. Roll out dough, dusting with flour as needed, to a rectangle slightly larger than 16x12". Trim to 16x12". Cut into 12 squares (you'll want a 4x3 grid). Brush excess flour from dough and surface.

Lightly coat muffin cups with nonstick spray. Sprinkle squares with a total of ¼ cup sugar, dividing evenly, and press gently to adhere. Turn over and repeat with another ¼ cup sugar, pressing gently to adhere. Shake off excess. Lift corners of each square and press into the center. Place each in a muffin cup. Wrap pans with plastic and chill in refrigerator at least 8 hours and up to 12 hours (dough will be puffed with slightly separated layers).

Preheat oven to 375°. Unwrap pans and sprinkle kouign-amann with remaining 2 Tbsp. sugar, dividing evenly. Bake until pastry is golden brown all over and sugar is deeply caramelized, 25–30 minutes (make sure to bake pastries while dough is still cold). Immediately remove from pan and transfer to a wire rack; let cool.

Buying European or European-style butter is a must for successful kouign-amann. *Its higher fat and lower moisture contents make it firm but elastic, so it's easier to roll out and softens less quickly. And if that's not enough to justify the higher cost, it's more flavorful, too. We tested our* kouign-amann *with widely available Plugrá and Kerrygold, and both yielded excellent, super-flaky results.*

MIX AND FORM BUTTER BLOCK

WRAP AND CHILL BUTTER BLOCK

ROLL OUT DOUGH AND ENCLOSE BUTTER BLOCK

FORM AND PROOF

CARAMEL-DIPPED POPOVERS with CHOCOLATE MOUSSE

MAKES 10

CHOCOLATE MOUSSE

6 oz. bittersweet chocolate
(at least 70% cacao),
melted, slightly cooled

½ tsp. kosher salt

3 large egg yolks

¼ cup sugar

1 cup heavy cream, divided

POPOVERS AND ASSEMBLY

Unsalted butter (for pans)

2 large eggs

½ cup heavy cream

½ cup whole milk

1 tsp. kosher salt

¼ tsp. freshly ground black
pepper

¾ cup all-purpose flour

½ cup grated white cheddar

Nonstick vegetable oil spray

1 cup sugar

These savory popovers from the Mast Brothers chocolatiers in Brooklyn are made with cheddar cheese, which keeps the dessert from veering into overly sweet territory.

CHOCOLATE MOUSSE

Place chocolate and salt in a large bowl; set aside. Cook egg yolks, sugar, and ½ cup cream in a medium saucepan over medium heat, whisking constantly, until thick enough to coat a spoon, about 4 minutes. Pour over chocolate mixture and whisk until chocolate is melted and mixture is smooth. Let cool.

Using a whisk, beat remaining ½ cup cream in a bowl until soft peaks form. Fold into cooled chocolate mixture; cover and chill until cold, at least 2 hours. **DO AHEAD:** Mousse can be made 2 days ahead. Keep chilled.

POPOVERS AND ASSEMBLY

Preheat oven to 425°. Lightly butter 10 cups of a standard 12-cup muffin tin or two 6-cup popover pans. Whisk eggs in a medium bowl to blend. Bring cream, milk, salt, and pepper to a simmer in a medium saucepan; whisking constantly, gradually add to eggs. Whisk in flour, then cheese (no lumps should remain).

Divide batter among prepared muffin cups, fill remaining cups halfway with water, and bake 15 minutes. Reduce heat to 350° and bake until popovers are puffed, golden brown, and crusty, 20–25 minutes longer. Turn out onto a wire rack and let cool.

Just before serving, line a baking sheet with parchment paper and lightly coat with nonstick spray. Fill a large bowl with ice water. Bring sugar and 3 Tbsp. water to a boil in a small saucepan over medium-high heat, stirring to dissolve sugar. Boil, brushing down sides with a damp brush and swirling pan occasionally, until mixture turns deep amber. Set the bottom of saucepan in ice water to stop the cooking and firm caramel slightly (this will make it easier to work with when dipping popovers).

Working quickly and with 1 popover at a time, dip bottoms into caramel and set, caramel side down, on prepared baking sheet; let cool. (If caramel becomes too hard while dipping, reheat over medium-low heat to a workable consistency.)

Once caramel has set, mix mousse with a rubber spatula to loosen. Transfer to a pastry bag fitted with a ¼" pastry tip. Working 1 at a time, poke holes in tops of popovers with pastry tip and fill popovers with mousse.

CHOCOLATE-CINNAMON "BABKALLAH"

12 SERVINGS

The impressively decadent chocolate-cinnamon swirl in our babka-challah hybrid only looks complicated. Once the dough is done, this bread is no harder to make than a basic three-strand bread. Have any left over? Get ready for the ultimate French toast.

DOUGH

½ cup whole milk

1 ¼-oz. envelope active dry yeast

4 large egg yolks

1 tsp. vanilla extract

½ cup (1 stick) unsalted butter, melted, cooled, plus more

⅓ cup granulated sugar

1 tsp. kosher salt

3 cups all-purpose flour, plus more

FILLING AND ASSEMBLY

6 oz. bittersweet chocolate, finely chopped

⅓ cup (packed) light brown sugar

1½ tsp. ground cinnamon

All-purpose flour (for surface)

¼ cup (½ stick) unsalted butter, room temperature

1 large egg yolk

Granulated sugar (for sprinkling)

DOUGH

Heat milk in a small saucepan until warm. Transfer to a large bowl and whisk in yeast; let sit until foamy, 5–10 minutes.

Whisk in egg yolks, vanilla, and ½ cup butter. Add sugar, salt, and 3 cups flour; mix until a shaggy dough forms. Knead dough on a lightly floured surface until supple, smooth, and no longer shiny, 5–10 minutes.

Transfer to a large buttered bowl. Cover and let sit in a warm place until doubled in size, 1½–2½ hours.

FILLING AND ASSEMBLY

Mix chocolate, brown sugar, and cinnamon in a small bowl.

Turn out dough onto a lightly floured surface; divide into three portions. Shape each into a 12"-long rope. Roll out each rope to a 12x6" rectangle about ⅛" thick. Brush with butter and top with chocolate mixture, pressing gently. Roll up to form a log; pinch seam to seal.

Place logs, seam side down, side by side on a parchment-lined baking sheet. Pinch logs together at one end; braid, then pinch ends together and tuck under. Cover loosely and let sit in a warm place until 1½ times larger, 1–2 hours.

Preheat oven to 350°. Beat egg yolk with 1 Tbsp. water in a small bowl. Brush dough with egg wash; sprinkle with granulated sugar. Bake until top is golden brown and "Babkallah" sounds hollow when bottom is tapped, 35–45 minutes. Let cool on a wire rack.

*Don't braid too tightly,
as the bread will expand during
the second rise.*

MEYER LEMON CREAM
with GRAHAM CRACKERS
and SEA SALT

4 SERVINGS

3 large eggs

⅔ cup sugar

2 tsp. finely grated Meyer or
     regular lemon zest

½ cup fresh Meyer or regular
     lemon juice

2 Tbsp. unsalted butter,
     cut into pieces

1½ cups chilled heavy cream

6 graham crackers, crumbled

     Flaky sea salt (such as Maldon)

Adding cream thins the lemon curd and makes it extra spoonable—delicious in more than just this dish. If you're using regular lemons, the curd will be a tad more tart.

Cook eggs, sugar, and lemon juice in a medium saucepan over medium heat, whisking constantly, until thickened (mixture should coat a spoon), 8–10 minutes.

Transfer mixture to a blender and blend on low speed, gradually adding butter, until mixture is smooth (you're not trying to aerate the mixture, so keep blender on low speed). Transfer lemon curd to a medium bowl, cover, and chill at least 2 hours.

Just before serving, whisk cream into lemon curd. Layer lemon cream and graham crackers in small glasses or bowls, finishing with graham crackers. Top with lemon zest and sea salt.

DO AHEAD: Lemon curd can be made 1 week ahead. Keep chilled.

3 More Ideas for Meyer Lemon Cream

The tart layer in this easy dessert is so good, you'll want to make it the base of other sweets, too. A few suggestions:

CAKE
Slather cream on a slice of vanilla pound cake at teatime (or snack time).

FRUIT AND CREAM
Layer in bowls with fresh fruit. Finish with a bit of raw sugar.

TART
Chill, then spoon into a prebaked tart shell, garnish with whipped mascarpone, and you've instantly got lemon cream pie.

ALMOND-BARLEY PORRIDGE with FRUIT COMPOTE

8 SERVINGS

COMPOTE
½ cup sugar

¾ cup dried cherries, divided

PORRIDGE
½ cup sliced blanched almonds, divided

4 cups whole milk

¾ cup pearl barley

½ tsp. kosher salt

1 vanilla bean, split lengthwise

3 oz. white chocolate, chopped

3 Tbsp. sugar

1 cup heavy cream

This fantastically creamy, not-at-all-healthy recipe is from Anders Braathen, head chef at Smalhans in Oslo. Live in a magical place where cloudberries (shown at left) abound? Lucky you! Use them instead of the dried cherries, as they do in Norway.

COMPOTE
Bring sugar, ½ cup cherries, and 1½ cups water to a simmer in a small saucepan over medium-low heat. Cook, stirring often and mashing fruit, until cherries start to fall apart, 15–20 minutes. Add remaining ¼ cup cherries and cook, stirring, until plumped, 5–8 minutes. Let cool. Cover and chill if making ahead (up to 1 week), but bring to room temperature before serving.

PORRIDGE
Preheat oven to 350°. Toast almonds on a rimmed baking sheet, tossing once, until golden brown, 5–7 minutes. Let cool.

Combine milk, barley, and salt in a medium saucepan. Scrape in vanilla seeds and add pod. Bring to a boil; reduce heat and simmer, stirring often and adding a little water if mixture gets too thick before barley is cooked, until barley is very tender and porridge is the consistency of oatmeal, 40–50 minutes.

Add white chocolate and sugar off heat, stirring to melt chocolate and dissolve sugar. Let cool. Remove vanilla pod.

Whisk cream in a large bowl to soft peaks. Fold into porridge in 2 additions; stir in half of almonds. Serve topped with compote and remaining almonds.

FROZEN CHOCOLATE
MOUSSE with CHERRY SAUCE

8 SERVINGS

MOUSSE
- ½ tsp. unflavored gelatin
- 5 large egg yolks
- ¼ tsp. kosher salt
- ¼ cup light corn syrup
- 3 Tbsp. sugar
- 6 oz. bittersweet or semisweet chocolate, melted, slightly cooled
- 1¼ cups heavy cream
- ⅓ cup coarsely chopped unsalted, roasted pistachios

SOUR CHERRY SAUCE
- 1 cup dried tart cherries
- 1 cup pure cherry juice
- ½ cup sugar

TOPPING AND ASSEMBLY
- ¾ cup chilled heavy cream
- ½ cup crème fraîche
- 2 Tbsp. sugar
- Pinch of kosher salt
- ½ vanilla bean, split lengthwise

SPECIAL EQUIPMENT: A candy thermometer

Slice this decadently rich and creamy terrine into portions and freeze on a parchment-lined baking sheet the day of the party; serving dessert will be a cinch. This recipe comes from chef Naomi Pomeroy in Portland, Oregon.

MOUSSE

Line an 8½x4½" loaf pan with plastic wrap, leaving a generous overhang on all sides; smooth plastic to avoid lines in finished mousse. Place 1 Tbsp. water in a small bowl. Sprinkle gelatin over and let sit 5 minutes.

Using an electric mixer on high speed, beat egg yolks and salt in a large bowl until pale yellow and frothy, about 4 minutes.

Fit a small saucepan with thermometer and bring corn syrup, sugar, and ¼ cup water to a boil. Cook until thermometer registers 238°. Remove from heat and add gelatin, stirring to dissolve. With mixer on medium-low, drizzle syrup into egg mixture. Mix in chocolate.

Using electric mixer with clean beaters, beat cream in a medium bowl to soft peaks. Mix one-third whipped cream into egg mixture. Fold in pistachios, then remaining whipped cream. Scrape mousse into prepared pan; cover tightly with plastic wrap. Freeze until solid, at least 5 hours.

DO AHEAD: Mousse can be frozen 4 days ahead. Keep frozen.

SOUR CHERRY SAUCE

Combine cherries and 2 cups very hot water in a small bowl; let sit 10 minutes to soften.

Meanwhile, bring cherry juice, sugar, and ½ cup water to a boil in a small saucepan over medium-high heat. Reduce heat. Drain cherries and add to saucepan; simmer until sugar is dissolved and mixture is slightly thickened, 8–12 minutes. Let cool.

DO AHEAD: Cherry sauce can be made 3 days ahead. Cover and chill. Bring to room temperature before using.

TOPPING AND ASSEMBLY

Combine cream, crème fraîche, sugar, and salt in a medium bowl. Scrape in seeds from vanilla bean; discard pod. Beat to soft peaks.

Let mousse thaw 5–10 minutes, then unmold, unwrap, and slice with a hot knife. Serve with cherry sauce and topping.

DO AHEAD: Topping can be made 30 minutes ahead. Cover and chill.

GOLDEN CASHEW-CURRY BRITTLE

8 SERVINGS

Nonstick vegetable oil spray

1 cup cashews

⅓ cup sugar

¼ cup light corn syrup

1 tsp. kosher salt

¾ tsp. curry powder

1 Tbsp. unsalted butter

¾ tsp. baking soda

SPECIAL EQUIPMENT: A candy thermometer; latex or other food-grade disposable gloves

Everyone loves brittle, which is why homemade presents like this from San Francisco's Craftsman and Wolves rule. (Just layer it between sheets of parchment or wax paper in small boxes.)

Preheat oven to 350°. Lightly coat a silicone baking mat or parchment paper with nonstick spray. Toast cashews on an unlined rimmed baking sheet, tossing once, until just beginning to brown, 5–8 minutes. Let cool.

Meanwhile, bring sugar, corn syrup, and ¼ cup water to a boil in a medium saucepan fitted with a thermometer over medium-high heat, stirring to dissolve sugar. Boil, swirling pan occasionally (at this point, you do not want to stir; doing so could encourage the sugar to crystallize), until thermometer registers 230°.

Add salt, curry powder, and cashews and stir, making sure cashews are completely coated and spices are evenly combined. Continue to cook, stirring constantly, until thermometer registers 300° (caramel will be a deep golden brown and cashews will be completely toasted).

Remove from heat and carefully stir in butter and baking soda; caramel will bubble and foam.

Immediately pour mixture onto prepared baking mat and let cool slightly. Wearing gloves (maybe even two pairs—mixture will be extremely hot), lift up an edge of baking mat and use it to fold mixture onto itself as if you were going to knead it; continue working in this fashion 1 minute. This will distribute the heat and incorporate air, resulting in a thin, crackly consistency.

As soon as mixture begins to firm up, stretch out, making it thin in places, but keeping it in one piece. (If today is not your day to sculpt molten sugar, simply pour mixture onto prepared sheet and use a spatula to spread it as thin as you can.) Let cool, then break brittle into uneven pieces, whatever size you like.

DO AHEAD: Brittle will keep airtight at room temperature up to 1 week.

The thin, shatteringly crisp consistency of this brittle is what sets it apart. The key? Kneading and stretching it while hot. Watch how at bonappetit.com/holidays.

CHOCOLATE FUDGE
with BOURBON SUGAR

MAKES 32

BOURBON SUGAR

1 vanilla bean, split lengthwise

1 cup demerara sugar

2 Tbsp. bourbon

FUDGE

Nonstick vegetable oil spray

10 oz. bittersweet chocolate (preferably 72%), coarsely chopped

4 oz. unsweetened chocolate, coarsely chopped

1 14-oz. can sweetened condensed milk

10 Tbsp. (1¼ sticks) unsalted butter, cut into pieces

2 Tbsp. bourbon

1 Tbsp. light corn syrup

¼ tsp. kosher salt

1 vanilla bean, split lengthwise

Flaky sea salt (such as Maldon)

This recipe makes more bourbon sugar than you'll need, and that's a good thing. Use it to top tea cakes and sprinkle over cookies before baking or to sweeten your morning coffee (we won't tell).

The exceptional texture and glossy sheen of this fudge from San Francisco's Craftsman and Wolves result from the way you mix it. Make sure the chocolate and condensed milk are barely hot.

BOURBON SUGAR

Preheat oven to 150° or as low as yours will go. Scrape vanilla seeds into a small bowl; stir in demerara sugar and bourbon. Spread on a parchment-lined baking sheet and let dry out in oven overnight, leaving door slightly ajar. Mixture should feel like demerara sugar again in the morning.

DO AHEAD: Store bourbon sugar airtight at room temperature up to 2 months.

FUDGE

Line an 8x8" baking dish with parchment paper, leaving a generous overhang on 2 sides; lightly coat with nonstick spray. Heat chocolates in a heatproof bowl set over a saucepan of simmering water (do not let bowl touch water), stirring occasionally, until almost completely melted. Set aside.

Combine condensed milk, butter, bourbon, corn syrup, and kosher salt in a small saucepan; scrape in vanilla seeds and add pod. Heat over medium until barely hot (same as the chocolate).

Gently stir one quarter of milk mixture into chocolate with a rubber spatula. Add another quarter of milk mixture, stirring to incorporate (it might look broken and greasy; don't worry, it will come back together). Continue with remaining milk mixture in 2 additions, stirring vigorously until fudge is very shiny and almost elastic, about 5 minutes. Scrape into prepared pan and smooth top. Sprinkle with bourbon sugar and sea salt. Let cool, then cover and chill at least 4 hours.

Turn out fudge onto a cutting board and slice into 2x¾" rectangles, 2" squares, or triangles.

DO AHEAD: Fudge can be made 1 week ahead. Wrap tightly and chill.

snacks & drinks

SWEET and TANGY HUMMUS

8 SERVINGS

1 15.5-oz. can chickpeas, rinsed

⅓ cup tahini

3 Tbsp. fresh lemon juice

1½ Tbsp. Turkish or Syrian red pepper paste or 2 tsp. harissa paste

1 Tbsp. pomegranate molasses (optional)

Kosher salt

Olive oil, Aleppo pepper or crushed red pepper flakes, and warm pita bread (for serving)

Red pepper paste gives this garlic-free hummus its color and smoky-sweet flavor; find it in Middle Eastern markets or online, along with pomegranate molasses.

Set aside 2 Tbsp. chickpeas for serving. Process tahini, lemon juice, red pepper paste, pomegranate molasses (if using), and remaining chickpeas in a food processor, adding water as needed, until hummus is very smooth; season with salt.

Serve hummus drizzled with oil and topped with Aleppo pepper and reserved chickpeas, with pita bread alongside.

DO AHEAD: Hummus can be made 3 days ahead. Cover and chill.

SMOKED SALMON TARTINES with FRIED CAPERS

4 SERVINGS

½ small red onion, very thinly sliced

⅔ cup Champagne vinegar or white wine vinegar

¼ cup vegetable oil

2 Tbsp. capers, rinsed, patted dry

8 slices country-style bread, toasted or grilled

1 cup crème fraîche

Kosher salt, freshly ground black pepper

1 lb. hot-smoked salmon, flaked

1 Tbsp. chopped fresh chives

Olive oil (for drizzling)

Find hot-smoked salmon, a Pacific Northwest delicacy, at specialty grocers. The Whale Wins chef Renee Erickson's favorite brand is available at lokifish.com.

Toss onion and vinegar in a small bowl; let stand at least 1 hour to pickle.

Heat oil in a small skillet over medium-high heat. Working in 2 batches, fry capers until opened and crisp, about 30 seconds. Drain on paper towels.

Spread toasts with crème fraîche and season with salt and pepper. Top with smoked salmon, drained pickled red onion, fried capers, and chives; drizzle with oil.

DO AHEAD: Onion can be pickled 1 day ahead. Cover and chill.

THE RESTAURANT BEHIND THE RECIPE

The Whale Wins

The Whale Wins is chef Renee Erickson's follow-up to her tiny spot The Walrus and The Carpenter, which landed on *Bon Appétit*'s list of America's Best New Restaurants back in 2011. You'll now find her in an airy, bright dining room in the Wallingford neighborhood of Seattle, serving rustic, wood-fired dishes driven by the bounty of the Pacific Northwest. Just across the hallway is the hip, well-lit Joule, whose chef, Rachel Yang, was doing the Korean-American mashup thing long before it became a national trend. Each woman's place is a standout on its own, but combined, they're the ideal restaurant: a little bit country cool and a little bit city chic.

BEET-FILLED EGGS

8 SERVINGS

2 medium red beets, scrubbed

1 garlic clove, finely grated

½ cup Parsley Mayo (see recipe below)

⅓ cup walnuts, coarsely chopped

¼ cup prunes, chopped

2 Tbsp. fresh lemon juice

Kosher salt

¾ cup store-bought pickled beets, finely chopped

8 hard-boiled large eggs

1 small golden beet, peeled, halved, thinly sliced

When you make this colorful, decadent, and profoundly flavorful appetizer from Kachka in Portland, Oregon, save the hard-boiled egg yolks, sieve them, and use them as a topping for caviar. Vodka shots not optional!

Preheat oven to 375°. Wrap red beets in foil and roast directly on the rack until a knife slides easily through the center, 1½–2 hours; let cool. Rub off skins with a paper towel; coarsely chop.

Pulse chopped red beets, garlic, Parsley Mayo, walnuts, prunes, and lemon juice in a food processor until smooth; season with salt. Stir in pickled beets. Place in a disposable pastry bag or resealable plastic bag.

Halve eggs lengthwise; remove yolks. Cut a ¾" opening in tip of pastry bag. Pipe filling into eggs, mounding slightly. Top each with a golden beet slice.

DO AHEAD: Beet filling can be made 1 day ahead. Chill in pastry bag.

PARSLEY MAYO

MAKES ABOUT 2 CUPS

1½ cups (packed) fresh parsley leaves

1½ cups mayonnaise

2 Tbsp. mustard

Kosher salt and freshly ground black pepper

At Portland's Kachka, they make mayo from scratch. But Hellmann's (a.k.a. Best Foods) will do just fine.

Pulse parsley, mayonnaise, and mustard in a food processor until smooth; season with salt and pepper.

SPICED SWEET POTATO and ROASTED BROCCOLI TOASTS

8 SERVINGS

SWEET POTATO MASH

- 1 large sweet potato (about 12 oz.), peeled, cut into 1" pieces
- 1 red Thai chile (optional), halved, some seeds removed
- ½ cup fresh orange juice

  Kosher salt, freshly ground black pepper

BROCCOLI AND ASSEMBLY

- 1 large head broccoli, stem removed, cut into large florets
- 8 Tbsp. olive oil, divided

  Kosher salt, freshly ground black pepper

- 4 ¾"-thick slices crusty bread
- 2 Tbsp. chopped raw pistachios
- 1 Tbsp. (or more) fresh lemon juice
- 1 Tbsp. chopped fresh basil, divided
- 1 Tbsp. chopped fresh mint, divided

  Flaky sea salt (such as Maldon)

The broccoli can be cooked early in the day (the sweet potato mash can be made days before), but toast the bread just before assembling so it doesn't dry out, says New York City chef Dan Kluger.

SWEET POTATO MASH

Combine sweet potato, chile (if using), orange juice, and 1 cup water in a small saucepan; season with salt and pepper. Bring to a boil, reduce heat, and simmer until sweet potato is very soft and liquid has evaporated, 20–25 minutes. Remove from heat and mash. Let cool slightly.

DO AHEAD: Sweet potato mash can be made 3 days ahead. Cover and chill.

BROCCOLI AND ASSEMBLY

Preheat oven to 425°. Toss broccoli and 2 Tbsp. oil on a rimmed baking sheet; season with salt and pepper. Roast until tender, 15–20 minutes. Let cool, then coarsely chop.

Meanwhile, brush both sides of bread with 2 Tbsp. oil total and toast on a baking sheet until golden brown, 6–8 minutes.

Toss broccoli, nuts, lemon juice, half of basil and mint, and remaining 4 Tbsp. oil in a large bowl; season with salt and pepper.

Spread toasts with sweet potato, top with broccoli mixture and remaining basil and mint, and sprinkle with sea salt. Cut into pieces.

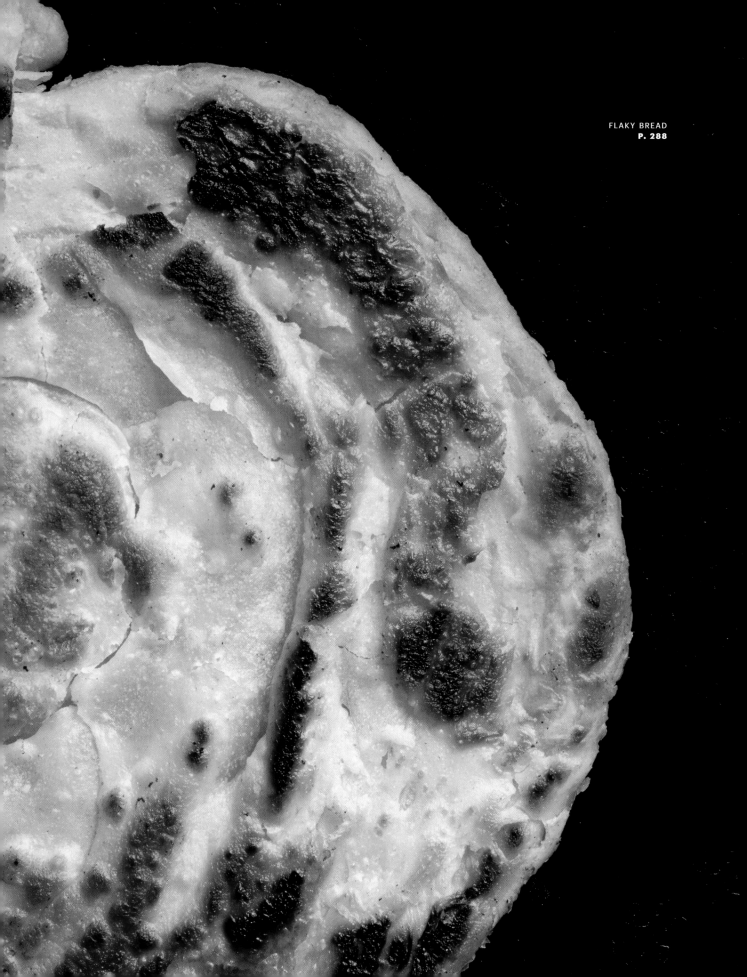

FLAKY BREAD
P. 288

SPICED
LABNEH
P. 289

CHARRED
EGGPLANT AND
TAHINI SPREAD
P. 289

HERBED
FETA DIP
P. 289

FLAKY BREAD

MAKES 10

1 tsp. kosher salt

3 cups all-purpose flour, plus more
   for surface

6 Tbsp. unsalted butter, melted,
   plus more, room temperature,
   for brushing (about 10 Tbsp.)

   Olive oil (for parchment)

   Flaky sea salt (such as Maldon)

This warm, buttery, pull-apart flaky bread is easy to throw together, crazy versatile, and can be made ahead and frozen. We're hooked! An unfloured surface provides some traction, so it's easy to roll the dough very thin.

Whisk kosher salt and 3 cups flour in a large bowl. Drizzle in melted butter; mix well. Gradually mix in ¾ cup water. Knead on a lightly floured surface until dough is shiny and very soft, about 5 minutes. Wrap in plastic; let rest in a warm spot at least 4 hours.

Divide dough into 10 pieces and, using your palm, roll into balls. Place balls on a baking sheet, cover with plastic wrap, and let rest 15 minutes.

Roll dough into thin rounds, brush with room-temperature butter, and roll up into ropes (see step-by-step instructions, below). Working with 1 coil at a time, roll out on an unfloured surface to 10" rounds no more than ⅛" thick. Stack as you go, separating with sheets of parchment brushed with oil.

Heat a large cast-iron griddle or skillet over medium-high heat. Working 1 at a time, brush both sides of a dough round with room-temperature butter and cook until lightly blistered and cooked through, about 2 minutes per side. Transfer bread to a wire rack and sprinkle with sea salt.

DO AHEAD: Coils can be rolled out 1 month ahead; wrap tightly and freeze. Cook from frozen (add 1–2 minutes to cooking time).

LAYER UP!

It's the buttery layers that set flaky bread apart from all others. To get them, nail this key coiling move.

1
ROLL
Using a rolling pin and working 1 piece at a time, roll out each ball on an unfloured surface into a very thin round (or oval).

2
ROPE
Brush with about ½ Tbsp. butter and sprinkle with flaky sea salt. Roll up dough onto itself to create a long, thin rope.

3
COIL
Wind the rope into a tight coil, then roll out again. The rolled-out coil will separate into thin, individual layers. Hello, flaky bread.

SPICED LABNEH

MAKES 1 CUP

1 cup labneh (Lebanese strained yogurt)

¼ tsp. ground allspice

1½ tsp. Aleppo pepper, plus more for serving

Kosher salt and freshly ground black pepper

Olive oil

Up the ante on your usual dip with this spicy Middle Eastern version.

Whisk labneh, allspice, and 1½ tsp. Aleppo pepper in a medium bowl; season with salt and black pepper. Drizzle with oil and top with more Aleppo pepper.

CHARRED EGGPLANT and TAHINI SPREAD

MAKES 1½ CUPS

1 large eggplant, cut lengthwise into quarters

¼ cup olive oil, plus more for drizzling

Kosher salt and freshly ground black pepper

1 garlic clove, finely grated

1 tsp. finely grated lemon zest

1 Tbsp. fresh lemon juice

1 Tbsp. tahini (sesame seed paste)

¾ tsp. ground cumin

Toasted sesame seeds

Smoky and sweet, this spread is perfect with flatbread.

Preheat oven to 475°. Place eggplant on a baking sheet and toss with ¼ cup oil; season with salt and pepper. Roast until lightly charred and very tender, 20–25 minutes; let cool slightly. Chop eggplant (skin and all) until almost a paste.

Mix eggplant in a medium bowl with garlic, lemon zest, lemon juice, tahini, and cumin; season with salt and pepper. Drizzle with oil and top with sesame seeds.

HERBED FETA DIP

MAKES 1¼ CUPS

6 oz. feta

½ cup finely chopped fresh flat-leaf parsley

¼ cup finely chopped fresh mint

2 Tbsp. finely chopped fresh dill, plus torn sprigs for serving

Kosher salt and freshly ground black pepper

Olive oil

Delicious with Flaky Bread—or pita chips.

Blend feta and a splash of water in a food processor. Transfer to a medium bowl and mix in parsley, mint, and chopped dill; season with salt and pepper. Drizzle with oil and top with dill sprigs.

PROSCIUTTO, WATERCRESS, and FONTINA TOASTIES

8 SERVINGS

8 thin slices prosciutto (about 3 oz.)

8 ½"-thick slices Pullman bread

8 oz. Fontina cheese, thinly sliced

¼ cup trimmed chopped watercress

¼ cup unsalted butter, room temperature

The keys to achieving razor-edged triangles, according to Portland, Oregon, chef Naomi Pomeroy: Let the sandwiches cool slightly, then slice with a serrated knife.

Preheat oven to 350°. Bake prosciutto on a parchment-lined baking sheet until it darkens and shrinks slightly, 6–8 minutes. Let cool (meat will crisp as it cools).

Top 4 slices of bread with half of cheese, prosciutto (breaking to fit), watercress, then remaining cheese (it will bind as it melts) and bread; butter tops.

Heat a large skillet over medium heat. Working in 2 batches, cook sandwiches, butter side down, pressing firmly, until bottom is golden brown. Butter tops, turn, and cook until golden brown and cheese is melted, about 4 minutes. Transfer to a wire rack; let cool slightly. Remove crusts and cut each sandwich into 4 triangles.

DO AHEAD: Toasties can be cooked 2 hours ahead. Store uncovered at room temperature. Reheat before serving.

DUBLIN
ICED COFFEE
P. 293

DUBLIN
ICED COFFEE

MAKES 1

2 oz. strong cold-brew coffee

2 oz. stout (such as AleSmith
　　Speedway or Guinness)

1½ oz. Irish whiskey

¾ oz. simple syrup

½ oz. heavy cream

　Freshly grated cinnamon
　　stick (for serving)

A delicious mix of caffeine, dessert, and danger from Soda & Swine in San Diego.

Mix coffee, stout, whiskey, and simple syrup in a highball glass. Add ice to fill. Gently pour in cream so it gradually sinks into coffee; sprinkle with cinnamon.

TROUBLE in PARADISE

MAKES 1

2 Tbsp. honey

2 fresh basil sprigs

1 oz. bourbon

1 oz. Campari

¾ oz. fresh grapefruit juice

¾ oz. fresh lemon juice

2 grinds black pepper

Isaac Shumway's cocktails for Tosca in San Francisco are so good, people drink them well into the meal. This sweet-tart beauty gets its surprising edge from basil and black pepper.

Shake honey and 1 Tbsp. warm water in a small jar until honey is dissolved. Combine 1 basil sprig, bourbon, Campari, grapefruit juice, lemon juice, ½ oz. honey syrup, and pepper in a cocktail shaker. Fill shaker with ice and shake vigorously until outside of shaker is frosty. Strain into a rocks glass filled with ice and garnish with remaining basil sprig.

BLACKBERRY and
GINGER COCKTAIL

MAKES 8

½ pint blackberries

8 sprigs mint, plus more
　　for serving

1½ cups vodka

1 cup fresh lime juice

3 12-oz. cans or bottles
　　ginger beer

Set aside some of the muddled berry-and-herb mixture and top with ginger beer to make a nonalcoholic refresher.

Muddle blackberries and mint in a large pitcher. Mix in vodka, lime juice, and ginger beer. Serve over ice garnished with more mint.

SAGE
BROWN DERBY

MAKES 1

2 oz. rye whiskey

1 oz. fresh red or pink
   grapefruit juice

½ oz. fresh lime juice

¼ oz. agave syrup (nectar)

2 dashes bitters

1 fresh sage leaf

Grapefruit cocktails are great year-round, but the rye and sage make
this one especially wintry.

Combine whiskey, grapefruit juice, lime juice, agave, and bitters in a
cocktail shaker. Fill shaker with ice and shake until outside is frosty,
about 30 seconds; strain into a coupe glass. Slap sage leaf between
your palms until fragrant; float on top of cocktail.

CELERY TONIC

MAKES 1

1 celery stalk, chopped

1 Tbsp. sugar

1 oz. fresh lemon juice

2 oz. gin

   Lemon twist (for serving)

The herbal notes of gin pair well with celery in this refreshing
cocktail—and bonus points for the cool green color.

Muddle celery with sugar and lemon juice in a cocktail shaker, 1 minute.
Add gin, fill shaker with ice, and shake until outside of shaker is frosty,
about 30 seconds. Strain into a rocks glass filled with ice and garnish
with lemon twist.

PEACH, GINGER, and
BOURBON FROZEN COCKTAIL

4 SERVINGS

3 cups sliced peeled
   peaches, frozen

2 Tbsp. finely grated
   peeled ginger

6 oz. bourbon

3 oz. simple syrup

2 oz. fresh lemon juice

   Sage sprigs (for serving;
   optional)

For best flavor, head to the farmers' market for peak-season fruit.
Freeze in a single layer on a parchment-lined rimmed baking sheet
until solid before puréeing.

Purée peaches, ginger, bourbon, simple syrup, lemon juice, and 2 cups
ice in a blender until smooth and very thick (mixture will loosen
immediately once poured). Divide among glasses and garnish with sage
sprigs, if desired.

LEMON-GINGER BREW

8 oz. ginger, peeled, chopped

½ cup fresh lemon juice

⅓ cup agave syrup (nectar) or pure maple syrup

Drink this elixir straight, mix with muddled strawberries for a twist on pink lemonade, or add rum to make it a cocktail. Whatever you do, keep a pitcher handy at all times in summer.

Pulse ginger in a food processor to a coarse paste. Bring ginger and 6 cups water to a boil in a medium saucepan; reduce heat and simmer until reduced to 3 cups, 30–40 minutes.

Strain into a large jar and mix in lemon juice and agave; add more lemon juice or agave, if desired. Let cool; cover and chill.

DO AHEAD: Brew can be made 2 weeks ahead. Keep chilled.

SRIRACHA-LADA

MAKES 1

1 oz. fresh lime juice

2 tsp. Sriracha

½ tsp. Worcestershire sauce

Kosher salt

Mexican lager (such as Pacifico; for serving)

Lime wheel (for serving)

Think of this as an Asian-inflected Michelada with some serious kick.

Combine lime juice, Sriracha, and Worcestershire sauce in a salt-rimmed pint glass filled with ice. Top off with lager. Garnish with lime wheel.

To cut down on foam when filling a glass, gently pour beer over the back of a spoon. Less froth means more beer, and that's never a bad thing.

SANGRIA BLANCO

16 SERVINGS

2 lemons, thinly sliced

1 pink grapefruit, thinly sliced

2 cups fresh pink grapefruit juice

1 375-ml bottle Dolin blanc or
   dry vermouth

1½ cups Suze Saveur d'Autrefois

¾ cup pisco

¼ cup torn fresh mint leaves

2 750-ml bottles chilled Vinho
   Verde

A refreshing citrus sangria that gets bittersweet notes from Suze,
a French aperitif.

Mix lemon slices, grapefruit slices and juice, vermouth, Suze, pisco,
and mint in a large pitcher or bowl and chill at least 4 hours.

Add Vinho Verde to citrus mixture just before serving. Serve over ice.

DO AHEAD: Citrus mixture can be made 12 hours ahead. Keep chilled.

WATERMELON, LIME, and TEQUILA FROZEN COCKTAIL

4 SERVINGS

3½ cups watermelon pieces,
   frozen; plus wedges
   for serving (optional)

6 oz. tequila blanco

4 oz. simple syrup

2 oz. fresh lime juice

1 ½"-thick jalapeño slice, with
   seeds; plus sliced jalapeño
   for serving (optional)

So much better than your typical margarita, this icy concoction tastes
just like vacation.

Purée watermelon, tequila, simple syrup, lime juice, ½"-thick jalapeño
slice, and 3 cups ice in a blender until smooth and very thick (mixture
will loosen immediately once poured). Divide among glasses and garnish
with watermelon wedges and jalapeño slices, if desired.

CRANBERRY RUM PUNCH

6 SERVINGS

2 cups fresh cranberries

½ cup sugar

1 cup white rum

½ cup fresh lime juice

Mint sprigs (for serving)

We'd gladly serve this on Thanksgiving, too.

Bring cranberries, sugar, and 2 cups water to a boil in a small saucepan, stirring to dissolve sugar. Strain syrup into a pitcher; cover and chill. Set cranberries aside.

Add rum and lime juice to syrup; chill until cold, about 1 hour. Serve punch over crushed ice garnished with reserved cranberries and mint sprigs.

SAINT-FLORENT COCKTAIL

8 SERVINGS

HONEY SYRUP

¼ cup clover honey

ASSEMBLY

1½ cups gin

¾ cup fresh lime juice

½ cup Aperol or Cappelletti

Angostura bitters

Champagne or sparkling wine

8 lime wheels

Created by Portland, Oregon's Naomi Pomeroy, this easy-drinking aperitif is made slightly more potent with the addition of gin.

HONEY SYRUP

Combine honey and 2 Tbsp. hot water in a small jar; cover and shake to dissolve honey.

ASSEMBLY

Combine 6 Tbsp. gin, 3 Tbsp. fresh lime juice, 2 Tbsp. Aperol, 1 Tbsp. honey syrup, and 2 dashes of Angostura bitters in a cocktail shaker; fill shaker with ice. Cover and shake until outside of shaker is frosty, about 30 seconds. Strain into 2 chilled coupe glasses. Top off each with Champagne and garnish with a lime wheel. Repeat three more times.

prep school
_____

the pro tools that upped our game this year

Carbon-Steel Skillet

Lighter than cast iron and more versatile than nonstick, a carbon-steel skillet does the job of both—evenly conducting heat like a diner griddle and easily releasing even the most delicate fish. Its preseasoned surface gets better with age, and more important, helps anyone perfect her omelet game. That alone is enough to earn it a spot on a list of kitchen essentials. We love the seasoned skillets from Lodge.

These squeeze bottles are one of those pro tools that work just as well at home.

2
Bench Scraper

Our go-to for getting every last bit of bread dough stuck on the work surface, moving vegetables from cutting board to pot, or portioning gnocchi, rolls, and more. It's like having a (sharper) spatula attached to your arm!

3
Digital Thermometer

Each time you slice into a piece of meat to see if it's cooked, precious juices escape. A digital thermometer gives you a precise temperature reading in less time than it takes to pull that chicken breast off the grill or roast out of the oven. Plus, it's fun to play with.

4
Oven Thermometer

It's a fact of kitchen life: Most ovens lie. Another fact: Most baked goods are temperamental—10 degrees can mean the difference between flat, crispy cookies and perfectly round, chewy ones. The solution is simple: You need an oven thermometer! Even if you don't bake, that rib roast will thank you, too.

5
Plastic Squeeze Bottles

Plastic squeeze bottles are standard issue in restaurant kitchens, where chefs use them to keep sauces, cooking oils, and dressings within arm's reach. In the *BA* Test Kitchen, we decant big cans of olive oil into smaller bottles and keep them next to our stovetops, along with vegetable oil and sticky stuff, like honey and agave. Paper-towel collars absorb drips, and painter's tape is handy for making labels.

A wire rack in a rimmed baking sheet is always in play in the BA kitchen.

6
Wire Rack

A wire rack set in a rimmed baking sheet is the ideal landing pad for fried foods. And it's great for keeping pancakes or waffles warm in the oven—no soggy bottoms! Plus, there's no better way to cool a cake or rest a roast; the pan catches all the crumbs and drips.

7
Take-Out Containers

Sturdy and stackable with lids that fit like a leakproof glove, plastic take-out containers (a.k.a. deli containers) are perfect for storing prepped ingredients and leftovers. Order them by the stack—and don't forget to label and date what's inside with masking tape and a Sharpie for easy organization.

8
Fish Spatula

This baby's thin, sturdy, slightly offset blade makes it perfect for flipping delicate fish fillets and fritters. Call it a "fish spat" and gain some cool-kid chef cred.

9
Spice Mill

For speedy and uniform pulverization of toasted spices, you'll need a spice mill, like the Krups F203 Fast Touch grinder. The best way to clean it? Blitz a piece of bread in it and wipe out.

Let's give it up for the mini offset spatula!

10
Spider

The most-used tool in some kitchens rarely does what it was designed to do. Sure, a bamboo skimmer (or spider), that Chinese restaurant staple, skims foam while you're making stock. But as a mini-colander, it can't be beat for pulling short pasta from boiling water or retrieving blanched veggies. Best of all, it fishes out fried things from hot oil so well that it's hard to fry without one. What won't it do? Break the bank. Find one for a few bucks in a Chinatown near you.

11
Cazuelas

When Bobby Flay spent a day in the *BA* Test Kitchen, he reached again and again for the terra-cotta dishes called *cazuelas* (kah-SWEH-las). Why all the love? These lightweight vessels, ubiquitous in Spain, can go from oven to table, and come in a full range of sizes. (Plus, they're inexpensive and look great!) Flay, who favors the eight-inch size, uses them to roast mushrooms with garlic and shallots, sizzle shrimp or squid in chile-infused oil, and slow-roast salmon. We're hooked; now it's your turn.

12
Mini Offset Spatula

Its versatility knows no bounds, sweet or savory. It spreads, it flips, it scrapes. It's the tool of choice when transferring cookies to a cooling rack, releasing a cake from a pan, spreading icing onto sandwich cookies, and even flipping scallops or crisp, lacy fritters.

13
Digital Scale

We've been saying it for years: Just buy one already! Essential for bread baking, for which precisely measured ingredients are key, and super helpful when portioning freezer-bound meats. Bonus: Weighing your ingredients means no more washing measuring cups and spoons.

...and the 14 techniques that made us better cooks

Burn Your Citrus (It's Okay, Really)

A squeeze of citrus can take a dish from *meh* to memorable. But chefs like Amanda Freitag of New York's Empire Diner are upping the ante, transforming lemons and oranges with the power of fire. "Charring brings out bitterness and sweetness, and tones down acidity," says Freitag. "It's like you're creating a new, more complex fruit." She chars halved citrus facedown in a cast-iron pan, then squeezes the intensified juice onto roast chicken, whisks it into vinaigrettes, and mixes it with melted butter in a 1:2 ratio to drizzle over grilled fish.

HOW TO DO IT:

Heat a cast-iron pan over medium-high heat. Halve lemons or oranges (feel free to experiment with different varieties) crosswise; rub a little olive oil on the cut sides. Cook citrus, cut side down, until nicely charred, about 5 minutes.

Know When to Stem 'Em

To get maximum flavor (and minimum chewiness) from nutritional show-offs like sturdy greens, keep these techniques in mind.

TO STEM...

Fibrous kale stems are no fun to eat. To remove them, hold onto the stem and run your other hand down the length, stripping the leaves right off.

...OR NOT TO STEM

But don't discard tender Swiss chard stems! They add texture, take well to pickling, and can be sautéed in your everyday *soffritto*.

THE PRETTIEST POACH

Ever crack an egg into simmering water only to watch the white spread out and form wispy tentacles? Try this game-changing fix: Break one egg into a sieve set over a bowl. The watery outer edge of the white will drain through, leaving the thicker white and yolk intact. Then slip the egg directly from the sieve into the water; the white will firm up around the yolk, creating a smooth, compact package.

PERFECT WHITE RICE Seattle chef Rachel Yang likes her rice "chopstick-ready": sticky enough to hold together lightly, but with defined grains. To get that texture, rinse 2 cups of short-grain white rice (a.k.a. sushi rice) in a sieve set in a bowl, changing water as needed, until water is just slightly milky. Drain, then bring rice and 2 cups water to a boil in a medium saucepan. Reduce heat, cover, and simmer until water is absorbed and rice is tender, 8–10 minutes. Remove from heat; let stand 10 minutes.

SCALLION CURLS

Transforming scallions from the straight and narrow into wild, curly, enticing ribbons requires little more than a sharp knife and a quick soak in some ice water. Here's how we do it.

1

CUT...

Cut scallions crosswise into 2" pieces, then slice lengthwise—the thinner the better.

2

...AND CURL

Let sit in cold water for 20 minutes (or chill overnight). They'll curl up as they soak.

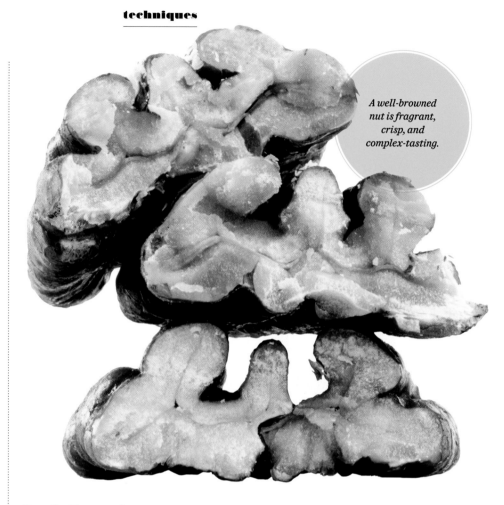

A well-browned nut is fragrant, crisp, and complex-tasting.

Really Toast Those Nuts!

Properly toasting a pecan—or any other nut, for that matter—will transform your dish. Not only does it intensify the flavor (especially important in the Chocolate-Caramel Pecan Tart, page 222), but it also ensures maximum crunch. A 350° oven is best for even and controlled roasting. And don't stop when the outside looks toasted—it's the inside that counts. After about 10 minutes, cut one open to check: It should be golden brown through and through. Oh, and burned nuts? That's an expensive mistake. Set a timer first!

VEGETABLE PEELER, MEET PARMESAN

No matter how sharp your blade is, it's nearly impossible to cut a hard cheese like Parmesan into ribbons with a knife. Instead, use your trusty vegetable peeler. Starting at one corner, create a flat plane by shaving off a few pieces, then continue—applying even pressure—to create inch-wide curls. If the shavings get too wide, rotate the cheese to a new edge and keep going.

Better Butter for Baking

"Shredding cold butter on a box grater is faster and easier than slicing cubes, and it makes those perfect mini bits that create fat pockets when scones bake." —*Jaime Sudberg, Beauty & Essex*

WHIPPED CREAM'S SECRET WEAPON

Powdered sugar! It dissolves instantly, and the little bit of cornstarch in it acts as a stabilizer, so you can whip it ahead of time and it won't deflate or get watery. Start by whipping the cream until soft peaks form, then beat in 2 Tbsp. for every cup of cream.

Lemon Twists

A well-crafted cocktail isn't complete without the right garnish. Here are three elemental citrus twists and how to master them.

BASIC TWIST
Use a vegetable peeler to remove a wide strip of zest with as little of the pith as possible.

THIN SPIRAL ZEST
Puncture the lemon with a channeling knife, a bar tool with a V-shaped blade. Firmly drag it around the fruit to create a long, thin spiral.

HORSE'S NECK
Trim the nubs from both ends of the lemon. Holding a sharp paring knife at an angle and starting at the top, remove the peel (and some pith), working your way around and down in an unbroken spiral. Apply even pressure and rotate the fruit, not the blade.

The Foolproof Grain-Cooking Method

This one-pot technique works for any grain.

PRESOAK Soaking slow-cooking grains (like farro and rye berries) in water overnight reduces their cooking time, makes them more digestible, and improves texture. Optional, but worth it.

BOIL LIKE PASTA Add grains to well-salted boiling water and simmer rapidly until done, which could take as little as 15 minutes for something bitty like millet or quinoa, or over an hour for a slow-cooking grain. Easy ratio: Cook 1 cup of grains in 6 cups water for 4 people.

TASTE AS YOU GO Cook grains till al dente: tender, but with some chew. As they simmer, taste them periodically (it's the best way to check). Use a fine-mesh sieve for draining—little beads of amaranth will pass right through a colander.

BONUS TRICK: TOAST FOR THE MOST Like searing a piece of meat or roasting vegetables till they're charred around the edges, toasting grains intensifies their flavor. Bake them for about 15 minutes in a 350° oven before boiling in our basic method (above).

what's new in our pantry

Chiles de Árbol

Grind them, use them in brines, or throw them into a pot of virtually anything—soups, beans, sautéed greens—for a hint of mellow heat.

HARISSA

A good cheat for the home cook because it's made with so many incredible ingredients, including chiles, olive oil, and a variety of North African spices.

ANCHOVIES

For saline depth. We especially love them with breadcrumbs on pasta. Try the Rustichella d'Abruzzo, Merro, or Conservas Ortiz brands.

ALEPPO PEPPER

A slightly sweet Syrian pepper with moderate heat. Use it to build flavor as well as finish dishes. Available at some specialty foods stores and from wholespice.com.

We love a little in our vinaigrette.

POMEGRANATE MOLASSES

The juice of sour pomegranates is reduced to make this sweet-tart syrup that adds a layer of complexity to everything from lamb kebabs to *baba ghanoush*.

GOCHUJANG

Gochujang, a fermented chile paste, is key in Korean food. Use as a condiment or a marinade. It just might become your new Sriracha.

VINEGAR

Beyond vinaigrettes, apple cider vinegar can replace lemon juice in bourbon-based cocktails. Sherry vinegar perks up a pot of beans or tomatoey stews.

SUMAC

This citrusy spice adds tart flavor and jewel-like color to dishes.

COLATURA

The Italian take on Asian fish sauce, this amber liquid is gathered from barrels of cured anchovies. Instant umami!

ZA'ATAR

This Middle Eastern blend of sumac, sesame seeds, and dried herbs is showing up on everything from flatbreads to grilled meats.

309

what's new in our fridge

Lardo

Bacon drippings improve even the humblest of dishes (braised greens, we mean you). And, thanks to *lardo*—fatback cured with herbs and spices—we can add porky goodness to just about anything. When thinly sliced, the pearly white ribbons melt in your mouth. Drape them over warm beans, or treat them as a decadent topping for bruschetta, flatbreads, and pizza.

TAHINI

Used in dressings, sauces, dips, even baked into flatbreads and cakes, nutty, silky sesame-seed paste is essential these days. Look for tahini that is smooth and light in color. The natural oil will rise to the top; stir to incorporate before using.

BUTTERMILK

Whether you use it in sweet or savory recipes—or even drink it straight—old-fashioned buttermilk has magical properties.

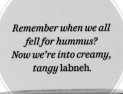

Remember when we all fell for hummus? Now we're into creamy, tangy labneh.

LABNEH

We spread the thick, Middle Eastern strained yogurt on bagels, freely dunk chips into it, and doctor a bowlful with olive oil and herbs as a veggie dip.

CULTURED BUTTER

When butter is the star—slathered on bread or baked into a flaky shortbread—we want one from cream that's been matured. That's what gives it a complex flavor and slight tang.

KIMCHI

This funky, spicy, crunchy fermented cabbage staple is enjoying its rightful place in the condiment canon. Our favorite is Tobagi Sliced Cabbage Kimchi.

UNSWEETENED ALMOND MILK

Of course it's a great milk substitute—it's high in protein and rich in omega-3s. But we also love almond milk—unsweetened organic, thanks—in creamy vinaigrettes, soups, and smoothies.

SCHMALTZ

Most brands render theirs with onion, lending an irresistible essence to whatever you pair it with. Use it to roast potatoes or to give a rich flavor to sautéed greens.

COCONUT WATER

Drinking Harmless Harvest is like sipping straight out of a fresh coconut: refreshing, thirst-quenching, completely satisfying. Pricey at $5 for 16 ounces, but worth it.

CLOUMAGE

Our favorite of the new *fromages*, this spreadable, American-made cheese is delicious anywhere you'd use chèvre or ricotta: in pastas, salads, frittatas, and sandwiches.

311

acknowledgments

When making a book like this one, there's no such thing as too many cooks in the kitchen. It takes an army of them.

Bon Appétit's executive editor, Christine Muhlke, oversaw the compilation of the book. Since she tastes every dish that goes into the magazine—often several times—she had plenty of ideas about which recipes, tools, and techiques should make the cut, and how it should all be structured. She also managed all sorts of other tasks, too lengthy to be mentioned here.

Designer Jody Churchfield worked tirelessly in a very short time period to make this tome as beautiful as it is.

Of course, the bread and butter of the book is the recipes, and every one of them is brought to you by the incredibly gifted, hard-working folks in the *Bon Appétit* Test Kitchen: food director Carla Lalli Music, senior food editor Alison Roman, digital food editor Dawn Perry, associate food editor Claire Saffitz, test kitchen manager Brad Leone, and recipe editor Liesel Davis.

Our recipes not only need to taste good, they need to look good, too. And that's where our art and photo teams come in. Our creative director, Alex Grossman, is the visionary who gives all of our

dishes that patented *BA* vibe (stylish but natural, delicious yet never precious). Photo director Alex Pollack oversees a freelance squad of hugely talented photographers. Many shoot regularly with us, and we are incredibly lucky to showcase their talents in this book: Ditte Isager; Taylor Peden and Jen Munk; Andrea Gentl and Martin Hyers; Michael Graydon and Nikole Herriott; Christopher Hirsheimer and Melissa Hamilton; Marcus Nilsson; and Danny Kim, to name a few.

We also depend heavily on food and prop stylists to make our food so alluring. We'd be nothing without our go-to food stylists Rebecca Jurkevich, Alison Attenborough, Susie Theodorou, Victoria Granof, and Susan Spungen. Our effortlessly chic prop stylists Kim Ficaro, Amy Wilson, Kaitlyn Du Ross, and Angharad Bailey are responsible for enriching our photos with all the beautiful vintage serviceware and stunning ceramic platters you wish you had in your kitchen.

Finally, one way or another, the entire staff of *Bon Appétit* contributed to this book—with all of their ideas, inspiration, and opinions that they share each and every week. We're very lucky to have so many amazing cooks in our kitchen.

credits

PHOTOGRAPHERS

William Abranowicz

Christopher Baker

Roland Bello

Julian Broad

Jamie Chung

Zach DeSart

Diane Fields

Gentl & Hyers

Michael Graydon +
Nikole Herriott

Hirsheimer & Hamilton/
Canal House Cooking

Christina Holmes

Ditte Isager

David Japy

Danny Kim

Eva Kolenko

Tuukka Koski

Alex Lau

Ryan Liebe

Jeremy Liebman

Ture Lillegraven

Jason Lowe

Charles Masters

Marcus Nilsson

Anders Overgaard

Peden + Munk

Christopher Testani

STYLISTS

Alison Attenborough

Lucy Attwater

Angharad Bailey

Sian Davies

Kaitlyn Du Ross

Kim Ficaro

Peter Frank

Lucy Harvey

Beverley Hyde

Rebecca Jurkevich

Kalen Kaminski

Christopher Lanier

Lisa Lee

Vivian Lui

Cyd McDowell

Elodie Rambaud

Ryan Rice

Christine Rudolph

Pamela Duncan Silver

Kendra Smoot

Susan Spungen

Susie Theodorou

Theo Vamvounakis

Amy Wilson

Chelsea Zimmer

RECIPE DEVELOPERS

Inaki Aizpitarte,
Le Chateaubriand, Paris

April Bloomfield, Josh Even,
Isaac Shumway, Tosca
Cafe, San Francisco

Nemo Bolin, Cook & Brown
Public House,
Providence, Rhode Island

Anders Braathen,
Smalhans, Oslo

Josef Centeno, Bar Amá,
Los Angeles

Matt Danzer and Ann
Redding, Uncle Boons,
New York City

Renee Erickson, The Whale
Wins, Seattle

Chris Fischer, Beach Plum
Restaurant, Menemsha,
Massachusetts

Bobby Flay

Ryan Hardy, Charlie Bird,
New York City

Hattie B's, Nashville

Anissa Helou

Takashi Inoue, Takashi,
New York City

Dan Kluger

Jessica Koslow, Sqirl,
Los Angeles

Lou Lambert and
Larry McGuire

Belinda Leong, B. Patisserie,
San Francisco

Mast Brothers Chocolate,
Brooklyn

Ignacio Mattos, Estela,
New York City

Paul McGee, Lost Lake,
Chicago

Carlo Mirarchi, Roberta's,
Brooklyn

Bonnie Morales, Kachka,
Portland, Oregon

Kristen Murray,
Mâurice Luncheonette,
Portland, Oregon

Alfia Muzio

Yotam Ottolenghi

Eleanore Park

Dawn Perry

Frank Pinello, Best Pizza,
Brooklyn

Naomi Pomeroy, Beast
and Expatriate,
Portland, Oregon

Alison Roman

Claire Saffitz

Peter Serpico, Serpico,
Philadelphia

Soda & Swine, San Diego

Susan Spungen

Mona Talbott

David Tanis

Quealy Watson, Hot Joy,
San Antonio

William Werner,
Craftsman and Wolves,
San Francisco

Jody Williams, Buvette,
New York and Paris

Rachel Yang, Trove and
Joule, Seattle

WE'D ALSO
LIKE TO THANK

Belle Cushing

Liesel Davis

Scott DeSimon

Matt Duckor

JJ Goode

Andrew Knowlton

Julia Kramer

Cree LeFavour

Christine Muhlke

Carla Lalli Music

Alex Pollack

Meryl Rothstein

Joanna Sciarrino

Amiel Stanek

Julia Turshen

recipe index

314